A SNEAK
PEEK INTO THE
FUTURE

KAY ARTHUR
JANNA ARNDT

HARVEST HOUSE PUBLISHERS

EUGENE, OREGON

Scripture quotations in this book are taken from the New American Standard Bible®, © 1960, 1962, 1963, 1968, 1971, 1972, 1973, 1975, 1977, 1995 by The Lockman Foundation. Used by permission. (www.Lockman.org)

Illustrations by Steve Bjorkman

Cover by Left Coast Design, Portland, Oregon

DISCOVER 4 YOURSELF is a registered trademark of The Hawkins Children's LLC. Harvest House Publishers, Inc., is the exclusive licensee of the federally registered trademark DISCOVER 4 YOURSELF.

A SNEAK PEEK INTO THE FUTURE

Copyright © 2007 by Precept Ministries International
Published by Harvest House Publishers
Eugene, Oregon 97402
www.harvesthousepublishers.com

ISBN 978-0-7369-2036-0

Printed in the United States of America

15   16   17   18   19   20   21   22   /ML-CF/   13   12   11   10   9   8   7   6   5

CONTENTS

Unveiling a Mystery—
A Bible Study You Can Do!

UNVEILING A MYSTERY—
A BIBLE STUDY YOU CAN DO!

Hey! It's great to have you back at the Discovery Bible Museum. Molly and I can't wait to continue our great mystery adventure in Revelation that we started in *Bible Prophecy for Kids.* By the way, my name is Max. Watch out for Sam (the great detective beagle). He has been waiting to give you a good face-licking. He gets so excited. You know how he loves these Bible adventures!

We have so much more to discover as we continue to unveil the mystery of Revelation. God put the book of Revelation in the Bible because it tells us the rest of His story. In *Bible Prophecy for Kids*, we saw WHO gave the revelation and WHAT the revelation is. We also uncovered the things John saw, the things that are, and began uncovering the things which will take place in the future.

The day of the wrath of the Lamb has come. Are you ready to find out WHAT happens WHEN the Lamb opens the seventh seal in Revelation 8? HOW many more judgments are there? WHO is the beast that comes out of the abyss? WHAT will happen to the two witnesses? WHO wins the battle of good and evil? And WHAT will heaven be like? We're going to see Jesus as we have never seen Him before: as the mighty Conqueror and Ruler of the world! *Wow!*

Revelation is an *amazing* book that shows us just how *awesome* God is! You can solve the mystery of Revelation by studying God's Word, the Bible, the source of all truth, and by asking God's Spirit to lead and guide you. You also have this book, which is an inductive Bible study. That word *inductive*

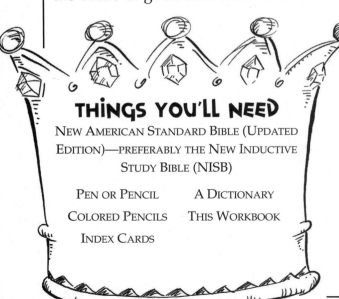

THINGS YOU'LL NEED

NEW AMERICAN STANDARD BIBLE (UPDATED EDITION)—PREFERABLY THE NEW INDUCTIVE STUDY BIBLE (NISB)

PEN OR PENCIL   A DICTIONARY

COLORED PENCILS   THIS WORKBOOK

INDEX CARDS

means you go straight to the Bible *yourself* to investigate what the Book of Revelation shows us about Jesus Christ and the things that must soon take place. In inductive Bible study, you discover for yourself what the Bible says and means.

Doesn't that sound awesome? Grab your Bible and art supplies and head back to the resource room so we can stir up our imaginations as we study God's Word. We'll experiment with some very cool exhibits to help you uncover the Bible's biggest mystery!

1

ANGELS SOUND THE TRUMPETS

REVELATION 6–10

Hey, guys! We are so excited that you're back. Molly and I can't wait to get started on our new adventure in Revelation 8 so that we can find out WHAT happens when the Lamb breaks the seventh seal.

In *Bible Prophecy for Kids* we unveiled an awesome mystery that God gave the Book of Revelation so that we would know what was going to happen in the future. As we got a glimpse into heaven at the things that haven't happened yet, we watched Jesus as the slain Lamb take a mysterious sealed up book and start breaking its seals. Amazing! We can't wait to find out what will happen next in heaven and on earth!

How about you? Are you ready to try out the rest of the cool exhibits in the Discovery Bible Museum and uncover the mystery of God's plan for the future? Great! Then let's get started.

THE LAMB BREAKS SIX SEALS

As you pull out your Bible, do you remember the first thing

you need to do before you ever start studying the Bible? That's right! You need to pray.

Bible study should always begin with prayer. We need to ask God to help us understand this great mystery of what is going to happen in the future. We want Him to lead and direct us by His Holy Spirit. Then we can understand what God says and make sure we handle His Word accurately.

Because the Book of Revelation reveals how God and Jesus triumph over Satan and evil, Satan will try to discourage us from studying God's Word and knowing the truth. So we need to pray and make sure we have our armor on. Read Ephesians 6:10-18 to help you remember what your armor is. Once we have our armor on, we will be able to stand firm against our enemy now and be prepared for the war against the Lamb (Revelation 17:14).

All right! Now that we have prayed and have our armor on, we are ready to go. But before we begin our new adventure in Revelation 8, we need to review WHAT happens in Revelation 6–7 as the Lamb takes the book out of God's hand and starts breaking the seven seals while some pretty scary events unfold on earth. We need to be sure we remember what happens as each one of these seals is broken before we solve the mystery of what happens next.

Turn to page 157. These Observation Worksheets are pages that have the Bible text printed on them. Read Revelation 6:1-2 to find out WHAT happens when the Lamb breaks the first seal. Underline the words referring to the <u>first seal</u> in orange and put an orange number 1 beside this verse so you can easily spot this seal as you look at Revelation.

Draw a sketch of this first seal on the chart on page 13. Make sure you add all the details (for example, if you are drawing one of the horses, show what the rider of the horse is carrying). And don't forget to fill in the blanks on your chart that describe this first seal.

Next, read Revelation 6:3-17. Underline the reference to each seal in orange and put the number of each seal beside the verse that refers to that seal. Then draw what happens for each seal that the Lamb breaks in Revelation 6:3-17. Fill in the blanks on the chart on page 13.

Great artwork! Now, let's read Revelation 7 on page 159 to see what else is happening during the sixth seal.

Revelation 7:1 WHAT did John see?

I saw _____ _____ standing at the _____ _____ of the _____, holding back the _____ _____ of the earth.

Revelation 7:2-3 WHY did the four angels have to wait before they could harm the earth, the sea, and the trees?

They had to wait until the _____-_____ of God were _____ on their _____.

Revelation 7:4 WHO are these bondservants of God that are sealed?

O _ _ _____ and _____-_____ thousand from every _____ of the _____ of _____.

HOW many from each tribe of the sons of Israel?

_____ _____ from each tribe.

There are two groups of people in Revelation 7. Let's look at the other group.

Revelation 7:9 WHO is this other group, and WHERE are they from?

A _____ _____ which no one could

count, from every _____ and all _____ and
_____ and _____, standing before the throne
and before the Lamb.

Revelation 7:13-14 WHERE have these come from?

_____

Did you remember the 144,000 and the great multitude from *Bible Prophecy for Kids?* Isn't it awesome that there will be believers who come out of the great tribulation? God will bring these people out of their suffering. The Lamb will be their shepherd, and He will guide them to the springs of the water of life. God will wipe every tear from their eyes. God has an amazing plan. He is a God of salvation!

Wow, what an awesome review! Six seals have been broken bringing about peace, war, famine, death, martyrs, and a great earthquake. The sun becomes as black as sackcloth, the moon like blood, stars fall to earth, the sky splits like a scroll, and every mountain and island are moved out of their places. People hide themselves in caves, rocks, and mountains. They cry out to be hid from the presence of God and the wrath of the Lamb. *Amazing!*

Did you remember that the breaking of these seals is the beginning of God's judgment on the earth? We know that God is a God of salvation. He is loving, forgiving, and merciful. But He is also a holy God who must judge sin. These judgments are coming to put an end to sin. God is the One who is in control over all these horrible events. He alone has all authority and power in His Hand!

Don't be afraid of these frightening events. If you belong to Jesus, you have nothing to fear. Jesus has already rescued you; your future is secure in Him.

Now, before we head back into the museum to experience the room that has the four angels standing at the four corners of the earth, we need to discover our memory verse.

To solve the mystery of this week's verse, look at the picture of the horses. WHAT is coming out of their mouths? Find the missing words in this week's verse by taking the words out of the smoke, fire, and brimstone, and putting them where they fit on the empty blanks below the horses. To help you solve this verse, we have given you the first letter of each word. Then find the correct reference and fill in that blank.

The rest of m __ __ __ __ __ __, who were not k __ __ __ __ __ __ by these p __ __ __ __ __ __ __, did not r __ __ __ __ __ __ of the works of their h __ __ __ __, so as not to w __ __ __ __ __ __ __ d __ __ __ __ __ __, and the i __ __ __ __ of g __ __ __ and of

s __ __ __ __ __ and of b __ __ __ __ and of s __ __ __ __ and
of w __ __ __, which can neither s __ __ nor h __ __ __ nor
w __ __ __.

Revelation 9:___

You did it! Now practice this verse so you will remember how
the rest of mankind reacts as God tries to get their attention.

THE SEVEN SEALS	
First Seal _____ horse Brings peace	**Second Seal** _____ horse Brings war
Third Seal _____ horse Brings famine	**Fourth Seal** _____ horse Brings death
Fifth Seal _____ under the _____	**Sixth Seal** earthquake, _____ , moon, _____ The great day of _____
Seventh Seal	
_____ in heaven, angels given _____ _____	

THE LAMB AND THE SEVENTH SEAL

"Good morning, Miss Kim," Molly called out as she headed into the resource room.

"Hey, it's great to have you two back," Miss Kim answered. "How did you enjoy visiting the room that had the four angels standing at the four corners of the earth?"

"I thought it was cool," Max replied. "I was surprised when Molly pushed the button and those huge fans started blowing like the winds. Then they suddenly stopped, so no wind could blow on the earth as the angel cried out from the rising sun."

"I liked the part," Molly joined in, "where we got to take rubber stamps and stamp seals on those 12 paper men that represented the 12,000 from each of the 12 tribes of Israel."

"Yeah," Max replied, "but holding those palm branches and dipping those little white pieces of linen in the red liquid, to represent the great multitude washing their robes in the Lamb's blood, was really the coolest. Kids are going to learn so much when they come here and get to do all these cool things in Revelation."

"I know, Max." Miss Kim smiled. "I get so excited just watching you and Molly try out these exhibits. Are you ready to see what's next?"

"We sure are," Molly replied.

"Then you need to get started on today's research. Max, why don't you pray? Then you can read Revelation 8."

All right! Now let's uncover the clues for Revelation 8. One way you can uncover clues is by looking for key words.

What are *key words?* Key words are words that pop up more than once. They are called key words because they help unlock the meaning of the chapter or book that you are studying and give you clues about what is most important in a passage of Scripture.

- Key words are usually used over and over again.
- Key words are important.
- Key words are used by the writer for a reason.

Once you discover a key word, you need to mark it in a special way using a special color or symbol so that you can immediately spot it in Scripture. Don't forget to mark any pronouns that go with the key words, too! WHAT are pronouns? Check out Max and Molly's research card below.

PRONOUNS

Pronouns are words that take the place of nouns. A noun is a person, place, or thing. A pronoun stands in for a noun! Here's an example: "Molly and Max are excited about their new Bible adventure. They can't wait to uncover the mysteries of Revelation!" The word *they* is a pronoun because it takes the place of Molly and Max's names in the second sentence. It is another word we use to refer to Molly and Max.

Watch for these other pronouns when you are marking people's names:

I	you	he	she
me	yours	him	her
mine	his	hers	
we	it		
our	its		
they	them		

To discover the main people and events of Revelation 8, you need to mark the key words below on your Observation

Worksheets at the end of this book. Remember, Observation Worksheets are pages that have the Bible text printed out for you to use as you do your study on the Book of Revelation.

You will also want to make a bookmark for your key words so that you can see them at a glance as you mark them on your Observation Worksheets.

So let's get started. Make your key-word bookmark by taking an index card and writing the key words listed below, as well as how you are going to mark them on your Observation Worksheets.

Then turn to page 162. Read Revelation 8:1-6 and mark the key words listed below on your Observation Worksheets:

God (draw a purple triangle and color it yellow)

Jesus (or any description that refers to Jesus like *the Lamb* and any pronouns) (draw a purple cross and color it yellow)

I saw (I looked) (color it blue)

throne (draw a throne and color it blue)

angel (draw blue wings or a blue angel and color it yellow)

seal (color it orange)

prayers (draw a purple and color it pink)

trumpet (sound, sounded, blasts when it refers to the trumpets) (color it yellow)

Don't forget to mark your pronouns! And don't forget to double-underline the WHERE in green and mark anything that tells you WHEN with a green clock or green circle .

All right! Now that we have looked for the obvious by marking our key words, we need to get the facts.

We need to ask the 5 W's and an H questions. What are the 5 W's and an H? They are the WHO, WHAT, WHERE, WHEN, WHY, and HOW questions.

1. Asking WHO helps you find out:
   WHO wrote this?
   WHO are we reading about?
   To WHOM was it written?
   WHO said this or did that?

2. WHAT helps you understand:
   WHAT is the author talking about?
   WHAT are the main things that happen?

3. WHERE helps you learn:
   WHERE did something happen?
   WHERE did they go?
   WHERE was this said?
   When we discover a WHERE, we double underline the WHERE in green.

4. WHEN tells us about time. We mark
   it with a green clock or a green circle like this:○.
   WHEN tells us:
   WHEN did this event happen or WHEN will it happen?
   WHEN did the main characters do something? It helps us to follow the order of events.

5. WHY asks questions like:
   WHY did he say that?
   WHY did this happen?
   WHY did they go there?

6. HOW lets you figure out things like:
   HOW is something to be done?
   HOW did people know something had happened?

Ask the 5 W's and an H to get the facts of Revelation 8:1-6.

Revelation 8:1 WHAT did the Lamb do?

_____

WHAT happened in heaven when the seal was broken?

_____

Is there usually silence in heaven? WHAT did we hear in heaven when we studied Revelation 4–5 in _Bible Prophecy for Kids?_ Praise. Now there is nothing but silence. Try turning everything off in your house and be still and quiet for five minutes. WHAT was it like?

_____

Do you think this silence is because something horrible is about to happen?

Revelation 8:2 WHAT did John see?

_____

WHAT was given to them?

_____

So WHAT is the seventh seal?

_____ for about half an hour; _____ angels given

_____ _____

Go back and draw this on your chart for the seven seals on page 13.

Then turn to page 162 and underline the seventh seal in orange and write the number 7 in the margin next to Revelation 8:1.

Revelation 8:3 WHO was standing at the altar, and WHAT was he holding? _____

_____

HOW many angels are there now? _____ angels

WHAT was given to this angel?

_____

WHAT was he to do with it?

_____

Isn't it awesome to see that our prayers are before the throne? God hears our prayers.

Revelation 8:4-5 WHAT did the angel do with the censer?

_____

WHERE did the angel throw it?

_____

WHAT happened?

_____

_____

Revelation 8:6 WHAT did the seven angels do when this happened?

_____

Can you imagine what this scene will be like as the censer is thrown to the earth and peals of thunder, sounds, flashes of lightning, and an earthquake happen on earth? And the seven angels stand ready to sound the seven trumpets!

We'll find out WHAT happens when these angels sound their trumpets tomorrow. Don't forget to practice this week's memory verse!

SILENCE IN HEAVEN

"Wow!" Molly exclaimed as she, Max, Miss Kim, and Uncle Jake entered into a room of absolute silence. "This is really weird. It's too quiet."

"It won't be for long." Uncle Jake smiled as he pointed to the seven models of angels holding trumpets up to their lips next to an altar holding a golden censer. "Go ahead, Max. Push the button in front of the altar."

Immediately peals of thunder came booming out with strobe lights creating flashing lightning. The floor shook while smoke and a red glow rose up out of the censer. "Oh, man!" Max exclaimed. "When am I going to quit being shocked when those buttons are pushed?"

Everyone laughed as Molly replied, "My legs are shaking. I'm not sure we should push the next button."

"Before you do," Miss Kim told them, "there's something you and other kids will get to do. They will get to come to this table over here and make a trumpet by taking an empty paper towel tube, painting it, and then blowing through it like a trumpet."

"Hey, I like that idea!" said Max. " I'm going to paint mine to look like brass. Then stand back! I bet I can blow really loud!"

You can make a trumpet too! Just ask mom or dad if you can have an empty paper towel tube. You can paint it and blow your trumpet as you remind yourself of what each of these trumpets represent.

Now head back to the resource room and find out what happens next. Don't forget to pray. Pull out your key-word bookmark and add the new key words listed below.

those who dwell on the earth   (color it green)

woe (circle it in black and color it brown)

Turn to page 163. Read Revelation 8:7-13 and mark your new key words and the key words listed below on your Observation Worksheet.

I looked   angel

trumpet (sound, sounded, blasts when it refers to the trumpets)

Don't forget to mark your pronouns! And don't forget to double-underline the <u>WHERE</u> in green and mark anything that tells you WHEN with a green clock 🕐 or green circle ⭕.

Now ask the 5 W's and an H for Revelation 8:7-13.

Revelation 8:7 WHAT happens when the first angel sounds his trumpet?

"There came _____ and _____, mixed with _____, and they were thrown to the _____; and a _____ of the _____ was _____ up, and a _____ of the _____ were _____ up, and _____ the green _____ was _____ up."

Look at your Observation Worksheet and underline the word *first* in brown. Now write the number *1* next to this verse to help you see when the first trumpet was sounded.

Turn to page 33 and draw a picture of the first trumpet.

Revelation 8:8-9 WHAT happens when the second angel sounds?

"Something like a great _____ burning with _____ was thrown into the _____; and a _____ of the _____ became _____, and a _____ of the _____ which were in the _____ and had life, _____; and a _____ of the ships were _____."

Now underline *second* on your Observation Worksheet and write the number of the trumpet next to the verse.
Draw a picture of the second trumpet on the chart on page 33.

Revelation 8:10-11 WHAT happens when the third angel sounds?

"A great _____ fell from _____, burning like a _____, and it fell on a _____ of the _____ and on the springs of _____." Verse 11: A _____ of the waters were made _____.

Underline *third* on your Observation Worksheet and write the number of the trumpet next to the verse.

Draw a picture of the third trumpet on your chart on page 33.

Revelation 8:12-13 WHAT happens when the fourth angel sounds?

"A _____ of the _____ and a _____ of the _____ and a _____ of the _____ were struck, so that a _____ of them would be _____."

Underline *fourth* on your Observation Worksheet and write the number of the trumpet next to the verse.

Draw a picture of the fourth trumpet on your chart on page 33.

Revelation 8:13 WHAT did John hear the eagle say with a loud voice?

_____

Way to go! You did a fantastic job today! Don't forget to practice your memory verse. Tomorrow we will find out why the eagle says, "Woe, woe, woe" as we watch the next three angels blow their trumpets.

THE FIFTH ANGEL SOUNDS

Are you ready for another exciting day in Revelation? Is it hard for you to believe that one day soon all these events will happen on earth? The beautiful earth we love will not look the same. One third of it will be burned up, the sea will be polluted, and the skies will be darkened—all because of mankind's sin. An eagle will fly in midheaven crying out "Woe, woe, woe!" What a sad day that will be.

Will it get people's attention? Will there be a change in the way they live? Will they finally turn to the one true God? Let's find out. Don't forget to pray and ask God to give you wisdom to understand.

Pull out your key-word bookmark and add these new key words:

seal (this is the seal that refers to whom God sealed, not the seven seals) (draw a purple S)

worship (circle in purple and color blue)

repent (draw a red arrow and color it yellow)

Turn to page 164. Read Revelation 9 and mark your new key words and the following key words on your Observation Worksheet.

God   I saw   angel   woe

trumpet (sound, sounded, blasts when it refers to the trumpets)

Don't forget to mark your pronouns! And don't forget to double underline the <u>WHERE</u> in green and anything that tells you WHEN with a green clock 🕐 or a green circle ◯ .

Now ask the 5 W's and an H.

Revelation 9:1 WHAT did John see when the fifth angel sounded?

_____

WHAT was given to him?

_____

Revelation 9:2-3 WHAT came out of the smoke upon the earth when he opened the bottomless pit?

_____

WHAT was given to them?

_____

Revelation 9:4 WHAT were they *not* allowed to hurt?

_____

_____

Go back to Revelation 7:3-4. WHO are these men who have the seal of God on their foreheads?

_____

Revelation 9:4-5 WHOM could the locusts hurt?

_____

WHAT could they do to these men who do not have the seal of God on their forehead?

_____

Revelation 9:6 WHAT will men seek and long for in those days?

_____

Will they die from these stings? _____

Revelation 9:7-10 WHAT did these locusts look like?

They looked like _____ prepared for _____.
On their heads were _____ like _____, and their
faces were like the faces of _____. "They had hair like
the _____ of _____, and their teeth were like
the _____ of _____. They had breastplates like
breastplates of _____; and the sound of their _____
was like the sound of _____, of many horses rushing
to _____. They have tails like _____, and
_____; and in their tails is their _____ to
_____ _____ for _____ months."

Revelation 9:11 WHO is over them, and WHAT are his
names?

They have as K __ __ g…the _____ of the abyss. His
name in Hebrew is _____. His name in Greek
is _____.

Did you know that both the Greek and Hebrew names
mean "a destroyer, a destroying angel"?

Revelation 9:12 WHAT has past?

_____

WHEN is the beginning of the first woe? WHAT trumpet
is this?

_____

The Greek word for *woe* is *ouai*. It is pronounced like this:
oo-ah' ee. It means an expression of grief. Have you noticed
that the judgments are intensifying, getting much worse
as they continue?

Revelation 9:12 HOW many woes are left?

_____

Underline *fifth* on your Observation Worksheet and write the number of the trumpet next to the verse.

Draw a picture of the fifth trumpet on your chart on page 33.

Revelation 9:13-15 WHAT happens when the sixth angel sounds?

I heard a voice say, "R__ __ __ __ __ __ the _____ angels who are _____ at the great _____ _____" so that they would k __ __ __ a _____ of mankind.

Revelation 9:16 HOW many were in the army of the horsemen?

_____

Revelation 9:17-19 WHAT did they look like?

"The riders had breastplates the color of _____ and of _____ and of _____; and the heads of the horses are like heads of _____; and out of their mouths proceed _____ and _____ and _____." The horses' tails are like _____ and have heads, and with them they do _____.

Revelation 9:20-21 WHAT do we see about mankind?

They did not _____.

Underline *sixth* on your Observation Worksheet and write the number of the trumpet next to the verse.

Draw a picture of the sixth trumpet on your chart on page 33.

Wow! Are you surprised that all of these horrible things are happening on earth, and it doesn't change the heart of mankind? Instead of turning to God and worshiping Him for who He really is, they just keep on sinning, worshiping demons and idols.

Have you noticed that God keeps using the word *repent?* To repent means to change your mind, to realize that what you are believing or doing is wrong according to God's Word. Do you see how important it is to change the things we are doing wrong (sin), tell God we're sorry, and then decide to do what God says?

Are you willing to do that? Ask yourself if there is anything that you need to confess to God, to stop doing or believing. Don't be like mankind in Revelation 9 who did not repent. Don't harden your heart. Ask God to forgive and change you!

Way to go! We are so proud of you!

A STRONG ANGEL

How did you like those locusts and armies of horsemen? Can you imagine creatures that look like that and have that kind of power? But did you also notice that they are limited in what they can do and whom they can hurt? Once again we see that God is in control over everything!

WHAT will we discover next? Let's head back to Revelation and uncover what John sees next.

Pull out your key-word bookmark and add the new key words listed below:

book (draw a brown scroll)

thunder (draw a black lightning bolt)

mystery (box it in orange and color it green)

Turn to page 167 and read Revelation 10. Mark your new key words and the key words listed below on your Observation Worksheet:

God   I saw   angel

trumpet (sound, sounded, blasts when it refers to the trumpets)

Don't forget to mark your pronouns! And don't forget to double-underline the <u>WHERE</u> in green and mark anything that tells you WHEN with a green clock 🕐 or green circle ⭕ .

Great work! Now uncover the mystery by asking the 5 W's and an H to solve the crossword puzzle on the next page.

Revelation 10:1 WHAT did John see?

1. (Across) I saw another _____

2. (Across) _____ coming out of heaven.

WHAT did he look like?

3. (Down) Clothed with a _____ , 4. (Across) and the _____ on his head, 5. (Down) his face like the _____ 6. (Down) and his feet like pillars of _____ .

Revelation 10:2 WHAT was in his hand?

7. (Across) A little _____ that was open.

WHERE were his feet?

8. (Across) Right foot on the _____,

9. (Across) left foot on the _____

Revelation 10:3 WHAT happened when he cried out?

10. (Across) Seven _____ 11. (Down) of _____
uttered their voices.

Revelation 10:4 WHAT did the voice from heaven say?

12. (Down) _____ up the things which the seven
peals of thunder had spoken 13. (Down) and do not
_____ them.

Revelation 10:6-7 WHAT did the angel say would be finished in the day the seventh angel sounds?

14. (Across) The _____ of God is finished,
as He spoke to His servants the prophets.

Revelation 10:8-9 WHAT did the voice from heaven tell
John to do with the book?

15. (Down) Take the book and _____ it.

Revelation 10:9-10 WHAT did it taste like in his mouth?

16. (Down) Sweet as _____

HOW did it make his stomach feel?

17. (Across) _____

Wow! WHO is still in control? _____. Were you surprised when God told John to seal up what the seven peals
of thunder had said? _____

God only reveals the things to us that we need to know. There are times when we won't know or understand God's plan.

Oh, the depth of the riches both of the wisdom and knowledge of God! How unsearchable are His judgments and unfathomable His ways! For who has known the mind of the Lord, or who became His counselor? Or who has first given to Him that it might be paid back to him again? For from Him and through Him and to Him are all things. To Him be the glory forever. Amen (Romans 11:33-36).

We have to remember to listen and obey the things God makes clear to us. When things aren't clear and we don't understand, we have to trust God. Remember God's character. He is a faithful God. He always keeps His promises! So…

Trust in the LORD with all your heart and do not lean on your own understanding (Proverbs 3:5).

You have done an *awesome* job! Now don't forget to practice saying your memory verse to a grown-up this week.

THE SEVEN TRUMPETS	
First Trumpet ⅓ third of the earth, _____ burned, all _____	**Second Trumpet** ⅓ third of _____ became b __ __ __ __
Third Trumpet ⅓ third of _____ and _____ bitter	**Fourth Trumpet** ⅓ of _____, _____, and _____ dark
Fifth Trumpet L __ __ __ __ __ __ from bottomless pit—_____ months torment _____ woe	**Sixth Trumpet** _____ angels at Euphrates k __ __ __ ⅓ of mankind. ____ million army _____ woe
Seventh Trumpet The _____ of the _____ has become the _____ of our _____ and of His _____. _____ woe	

2

SATAN IS CAST DOWN TO EARTH!

REVELATION 11–12

Wow! Last week was pretty exciting as we watched Jesus break the seventh seal and saw the seven angels who stand before God with seven trumpets begin to sound.

Just look at all the destruction that happens on the earth as the angels start sounding their trumpets. Does this destruction cause those who dwell on the earth to turn to God and repent? No! They just keep on sinning!

WHAT will happen next? Have all seven trumpets been sounded? Let's head back to the museum to find out what happens when the seventh angel sounds his trumpet.

DAY ONE

VOICES IN HEAVEN

It's great to have you back in the resource room! Are you ready for another action-packed week as we uncover the mysteries in Revelation 11–12? It's going to be quite an adventure! Why don't you get started by praying with Max and Molly? Then you can start uncovering the mystery of Revelation 11.

Pull out your key-word bookmark, Bible detectives, and add the new key words listed below:

two witnesses (and any synonyms that refer to them, such as *two olive trees* or *two lampstands*) (color it blue)

beast (color it brown)

make war (wage war, any reference to war) (circle it in black)

Turn to page 169. Read Revelation 11:1-14. Mark your new key words and the key words listed below on your Observation Worksheet:

 God   Jesus (Lord)   woe   worship

those who dwell on the earth

Don't forget to mark your pronouns! And don't forget to double-underline the <u>WHERE</u> in green and mark anything that tells you WHEN with a green clock or green circle ◯ .

All right! Way to go! Now solve the mystery of what happens when the seventh angel sounds his trumpet. Look at the mixed up message. It looks like it has been written backwards! Find out what the loud voices in heaven are saying by looking at the first line of letters. Start reading on the far right and write each letter from right to left on the first line. Then you need to do the same thing for the next three lines of letters to unscramble this verse and solve the mystery.

Great work! Now look up Revelation 11 in your Bible to discover the reference for your memory verse this week.

;dednuos legna htneves eht nehT
ni seciov duol erew ereht dna
fo modgnik ehT" ,gniyas, nevaeh
modgnik eht emoceb sah dlrow eht
dna ;tsirhC siH fo dna droL ruo fo
".reve dna reverof ngier lliw eH

_____

_____

_____

_____

_____

_____

Revelation 11:___

Don't forget to say it out loud three times in a row three times today!

DAY TWO

TWO WITNESSES

"Wait a minute, Sam! Don't eat that!" Max cried out. "Quick! Grab Sam! Don't let him get behind that cabinet, or else he'll be shredding that paper."

You did it! You captured Sam.

"Bad dog, Sam. You know you can't run off and eat paper! Miss Kim will make you stay home if you can't stay out of the art supplies," Max scolded. "Why do you love shredding paper?"

Poor Sam just sighed as he lay at Max's feet and gave him those big, sad beagle eyes. Molly laughed. "We better get started before Sam decides to find something else he's not supposed to eat."

Thanks for your help, Bible detectives! Are you ready to head back to Revelation 11? Don't forget to pray. Turn to page 169. Read Revelation 11:1-14. Let's ask the 5 W's and an H questions.

Revelation 11:1 WHAT was John given?

_____

WHAT was he told to measure?

_____

Is there a temple on the Temple Mount in Jerusalem right now? No. But from looking at Revelation 11, will there be one before Jesus comes back again? _____

Revelation 11:2 WHY isn't the court outside the temple to be measured?

_____

_____

HOW long will they tread under foot the holy city?

_____

Do you know how long 42 months is? This is a very important time phrase that we will see over and over again, as well as the time phrases "1,260 days" and "time and times and half a time."

HOW much time do these phrases refer to? The biblical

calendar only has 360 days instead of 365 days, so these time phrases of "42 months," "1,260 days," and "time and times and half a time" are different ways of saying the same amount of time. They are all a period of 3½ years.

Revelation 11:3 WHO is going to have authority granted to them?

_____

WHAT other names are these two witnesses called?

Revelation 11:4 Two _____ _____,

the two _____, and

Revelation 11:10 two _____

Revelation 11:3 WHAT will they be given authority to do?

_____

For HOW long?_____

HOW long did we discover that was? _____ years

Revelation 11:5 WHAT happens if anyone wants to harm them?

_____

Revelation 11:6 WHAT incredible powers will these two witnesses have?

1) They have the power to _____

_____

2) They have the power over _____

_____ 3) and to _____

_____

Revelation 11:7-8 WHAT happens to these two witnesses after they finish their testimony?

_____

_____

WHO killed the two witnesses?

_____

WHO is this beast? This is the first time we have met him in Revelation. We'll find out more about him as we continue our study!

Revelation 11:9 WHAT do the peoples, tribes and tongues, and nations do?

_____

_____

Revelation 11:10 WHAT do we see about those who dwell on the earth?

_____

WHY did they do this?

_____

Revelation 11:11-12 WHAT happens after three and a half days?

_____

_____

_____

_____

Wow! That's pretty amazing! Draw a picture of these two witnesses in the box. Show them prophesying, fire coming from their mouths, water turning to blood, and their deaths and resurrections.

Revelation 11:13 WHAT happens in that hour?

_____

_____

Revelation 11:14 WHAT is past?

_____

WHEN was the first woe? Do you remember? Look back at Revelation 9:1 and 9:12. _____

Revelation 9:13 WHEN do you think the second woe is taking place? _____

WHEN do you think the two witnesses are prophesying? During WHAT trumpet? _____

Look at the time line on page 54 and write *two witnesses* in the blank that shows where they should go on this time line, and write how long they prophesied. Also fill in the blanks that show where the three woes go.

You did a fantastic job! Tomorrow we will find out what happens after the two witnesses are taken up to heaven.

THE SEVENTH ANGEL SOUNDS

You did an awesome job yesterday sketching the two witnesses and their ministry on earth. Can you believe that those who are on the earth will actually send gifts to one another, rejoicing over the death of these two prophets? It is so sad to see how evil and corrupt those who dwell on the earth are during this time.

WHAT happens next in heaven? Let's find out. Pray. Now pull out your key-word bookmark and add the new key words listed below:

wrath (draw a red *w*)

kingdom (draw a purple crown and color it blue)

Turn to page 171. Read Revelation 11:14-19 and mark your new key words and the key words listed below on your Observation Worksheet. Don't forget you can turn to page 153 if you have lost your bookmark.

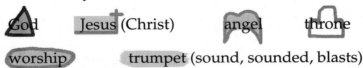

God   Jesus (Christ)   angel   throne

worship   trumpet (sound, sounded, blasts)

Don't forget to mark your pronouns! And don't forget to double-underline the <u>WHERE</u> in green and mark anything that tells you WHEN with a green clock 🕐 or green circle ◯.

Now solve the mystery by asking the 5 W's and an H questions.

Revelation 11:15 WHAT happens?

The _____ _____ sounded.

WHAT is this seventh trumpet? WHAT do the loud voices in heaven say?

"The _____ of the _____ has become the _____ of our _____ and of His _____ and He will _____ _____ and ever."

Isn't this awesome? We know that Christ defeated Satan when He died on the cross and was resurrected. Now we see the process of Christ beginning to reign in this world. The kingdom of this world will be conquered by the kingdom of Christ!

Now look back at Revelation 10:7 on page 168.

WHAT does it say is finished when the seventh angel is about to sound?

The _____ of _____ is finished.

Turn to page 171 and look at Revelation 11:15 on your Observation Worksheet and underline the word *seventh* in brown. Write the number *7* next to the verse so that you can easily see when the seventh trumpet is sounded.

Now go back to page 33, and draw a picture of the seventh trumpet on your chart of the seven trumpets and fill in the blanks.

Revelation 11:16 WHAT did the twenty-four elders do?

They _____ on their _____ and _____
_____.

Revelation 11:17 WHAT do they say?

"We give You _____, O Lord God, the _____, who are and who were, because You have _____ Your great _____ and have begun to _____."

Revelation 11:18 WHAT do we see about the nations?

They were _____.

WHAT came?

"Your _____ came, and the time came for the _____ to be _____, and the time to _____ Your _____-_____ the _____ and

the _____ and those who _____ Your
_____, the _____ and the _____, and to
_____ those who destroy the _____."

Revelation 11:19 WHAT happened in heaven?

"The _____ of God…was opened; and the _____
of His _____ appeared in His _____, and
there were flashes of _____ and sounds and peals
of _____ and an _____ and a great
_____."

Amazing! Now go back and find each one of the words from
your blanks (starting on page 42) in the word search below. If
a word is used more than one time, you only need to circle it
once.

B	O	N	D	S	E	R	V	A	N	T	S	D	O	G
K	T	H	A	N	K	S	E	C	A	F	A	G	D	K
I	N	V	A	H	A	I	L	S	T	O	R	M	P	T
N	A	X	T	H	U	N	D	E	R	G	K	Y	W	P
G	M	I	G	I	G	H	P	C	H	R	I	S	T	O
D	D	E	P	I	H	S	R	O	W	S	Y	T	S	W
O	G	N	I	N	T	H	G	I	L	T	O	E	E	E
M	R	E	W	A	R	D	R	O	L	E	R	R	V	R
E	S	E	D	A	A	L	M	I	G	H	T	Y	E	E
N	T	N	A	N	E	V	O	C	T	P	S	V	N	I
A	N	R	E	G	F	T	C	R	G	O	E	O	T	G
M	I	A	D	E	L	L	A	M	S	R	D	I	H	N
E	A	G	C	L	L	E	F	K	O	P	E	G	B	M
Y	S	E	L	P	M	E	T	F	E	W	R	A	T	H
J	U	D	G	E	D	L	R	O	W	N	N	Y	T	E

Way to go! While we see that the nations are enraged, we know the seventh trumpet has sounded and Jesus is on His way. Don't forget to practice your memory verse to remind you that Christ's kingdom is coming and that He will reign forever and ever!

TWO SIGNS IN HEAVEN

"That was so cool getting to go back inside heaven and hearing the loud voices as the seventh angel sounded, declaring that the kingdom of this world has become the kingdom of our Lord and His Christ!" Max said as he and Molly left the room in heaven to head back to the resource room.

"I just love hearing the 24 elders praise God. It is so awesome," Molly replied. "This is such an amazing place! I can't believe all the neat ways that we are getting to experience what happens in Revelation. Let's hurry so we can find out what happens next."

How about you? Are you excited about all you are discovering? Let's head to Revelation 12. Things are about to get really interesting! Don't forget to pray. Now do the research. Pull out your key-word bookmark and add the new key words listed below:

sign (draw a red sign)

woman (color it blue)

woman's child (box it in purple)

wilderness (color it orange)

Turn to page 172. Read Revelation 12 and mark your new

key words and the key words listed below on your Observation Worksheet:

 God   Jesus (Lamb)   throne

Don't forget to mark your pronouns! And don't forget to double-underline the <u>WHERE</u> in green and mark anything that tells you WHEN with a green clock or green circle .

Great observation! Now let's see what we can discover about this first sign in heaven.

Revelation 12:1 WHAT was the first sign in heaven?

A _____

Now that we know what the first sign is, let's make a list about this woman.

THE WOMAN

Revelation 12:1 Clothed with the _____, and the _____ under her feet and on her head a _____ of _____ _____.

Revelation 12:2 She was with _____. She cried out, being in _____ and in _____ to give _____.

Revelation 12:4 The _____ stands before the woman who was about to give _____, so that he might _____ her _____.

Revelation 12:5 She gave birth to a _____ _____, who is to _____ all the _____ with a _____ of _____. Her child was _____ _____ to _____ and to His _____.

Revelation 12:6 The woman fled into the _____

---

where she had a place prepared by _____ so that she would be nourished _____ days.

Revelation 12:13 The _____ persecuted the woman.

Revelation 12:14 The _____ _____ of the great _____ were given to the woman, so that she could fly into the _____ to her place, where she was nourished for a _____ and _____ and _____ a _____, from the presence of the _____.

Revelation 12:15 The _____ poured _____ like a river out of his mouth after the woman, so that he might cause her to be _____ away with the _____.

Revelation 12:16 The earth _____ the woman.

Revelation 12:17 The _____ was _____ with the woman, and went off to make _____ with the rest of her _____, who keep the commandments of God and hold to the testimony of _____.

Now that we have the facts about this woman, let's do some cross-referencing to see if we can figure out WHO this woman could be. Look up Genesis 37:9-10.

Do you remember this dream Joseph had about the sun, moon, and stars bowing down to him? WHOM did this dream represent?

_____

Genesis 37:2 WHO was Joseph's father? Do you remember? _____

Genesis 35:10 God changed Jacob's name to WHAT?

_____

Genesis 35:22 HOW many children did Jacob (Israel) have?

_____

These 12 sons are known as the 12 tribes of Israel.

Look up and read Matthew 1:1-2.

WHAT male child also came from one of the 12 tribes of Israel?

_____

Look up and read Matthew 28:5-6 and Acts 1:9-11.

Was this child ever caught up to God? _____

Look up and read Psalm 2:6-9.

Psalm 2:9 WHAT is God's Son going to do?

_____

Read Revelation 12:5. WHAT is the woman's son going to do?

_____

This same child is going to rule and reign with a rod of iron for 1,000 years in Revelation 20.

From what you have seen in God's Word, WHO do you think this child is? _____

WHO do you think the child's mother is? WHAT nation does this child come from? _____

WHAT does all this mean? We'll find out more tomorrow as we uncover what the other sign is in heaven. Keep up the good work!

WHO IS THE DRAGON?

Hey! Come on in. Are you ready to solve the mystery of the next sign in heaven? Are you amazed at how God has revealed this book to John with all these awesome images in heaven?

Don't forget to pray. Ask God to help you understand the things He has revealed so that you will know what is going to happen "after these things."

Now let's get started. Pull out your key-word bookmark and add the new key words listed below:

dragon (devil, serpent, Satan) (draw a red pitchfork)

was thrown down (has been thrown down, etc.) (color it green)

overcame (color it yellow)

Read Revelation 12 on page 172 and mark your new key words and the key words listed below on your Observation Worksheet:

make war (wage war, any reference to war)   angel

woe   wrath

Don't forget to mark your pronouns!

Now solve the mystery by asking the 5 W's and an H.

Revelation 12:3 WHAT is the second sign John sees in heaven?

_____

HOW many heads does this dragon have, and what was on his heads?

_____

HOW many horns does he have? _____

Revelation 12:4 WHAT did this dragon's tail sweep away?

_____

WHAT are these stars? Do you know? Look up Revelation 1:20 in your Bible.

WHOM do the stars represent? The _____

Revelation 12:4 WHAT did the dragon want to do to the woman's child?

_____

WHO did we discover this child is?

_____

Revelation 12:7 WHAT was going on in heaven?

_____

WHO was waging war with WHOM?

_____

Revelation 12:8-9 WHAT happened in this war?

_____

WHO is the dragon?

The _____ of old, who is called the _____ and _____, who _____ the whole world.

Did you know that Satan stands before God and accuses us day and night? WHAT does God see if we belong to Jesus? Do you know? He sees our sins—the things Satan accuses us of—covered with Jesus' blood. Satan accuses us, but God finds us not guilty because we have accepted Jesus, and His blood pays for all our sins. A big Bible word for this is *atonement*, which means all of our sins are covered.

WHERE do you think Satan, being cast down, would fit on our time line? Compare Revelation 11:15 with Revelation 12:10.

Do these passages sound alike? Do you think that Revelation 12:10 could be the seventh trumpet? _____

If so, turn to page 54 to our time line and add "Satan cast down" on the blanks under the seventh trumpet.

Revelation 12:12 WHAT happens in heaven when Satan is cast down to earth?

_____

WHAT does it say about the earth and the sea now that the devil has come down?

_____

WHAT does the devil have?

Great _____

HOW long does he have?

_____

Revelation 12:13 WHOM is the dragon going to persecute?

_____

HOW long do you think this could be? Look back at Revelation 12:6, and 12:14. HOW long is the woman going to be nourished away from the presence of the serpent?

_____

So we know that when the devil comes down, the woman runs and hides for 1,260 days, and "time, and times, and half a time," which we learned is 3½ years. This means that the devil is hanging around earth for 3½ years! Turn to page 54 and add 3½ years to your time line under Satan cast down.

Wow! Do you see how the process has begun? The kingdom of this world receives a direct attack as the war begins in heaven and Satan is cast down to the earth. There is great rejoicing in heaven because Satan no longer has access to heaven. But there is great woe on the earth and the sea because Satan will now unleash his wrath on the earth. Satan has been banished from heaven, and the war is on to restore the kingdom of Christ.

Don't forget to say your memory verse to a grown-up. This verse should make you feel like shouting. Praise God! His kingdom on earth is coming!

TiME LiNE

SEVEN SEALS

"After these things"— Rev. 4:1

Lamb breaks seals— Rev. 6:1

1	2	3	4	5	6	7
White horse	Red horse	Black horse	Ashen horse	Souls under altar	Sun moon stars earthquake the great day of wrath	Silence in heaven

SEVEN TRUMPETS

1	2	3	4	5	6
1/3 earth and trees burned and all grass	1/3 sea became blood	1/3 rivers & springs bitter	1/3 sun moon, stars dark	Locusts from bottomless pit—5 mos. torment	4 angels at Euphrates kill 1/3 mankind 200 million army
				___ woe	___ woe

Two ___ ___ years

The b ___

SEVEN BOWLS

7	1	2	3	4	5	6	7
Kingdom of this world has become the kingdom of our Lord and His Christ	Earth sores on those with mark of beast	Sea blood everything died	Rivers & springs blood	Sun man scorched	Throne of beast	Euphrates dried up	Air

___ woe
___ cast down
___ years

___ of God finished
___ falls

S ___ bound

Christ's ___-year reign

S ___ Judgment

Great Judgment

New ___ & new

3

THE MARK OF THE BEAST

REVELATION 13–14

It's great to have you back at the museum! Can you believe all the events that are unfolding on earth? Last week we saw some pretty amazing events. We saw the two witnesses of God begin their 3½ years of earthly ministry. We watched as they prophesied, sent plagues, and destroyed those who tried to harm them with fire. Then after 3½ years of ministry, we saw the beast come up out of the abyss and kill these two witnesses. WHO is this beast? HOW was he able to kill them? We'll find out more about him this week.

After the two witnesses, we saw two signs in heaven. While we looked at cross-references to discover WHO the woman and child are, God showed us exactly WHO this dragon is. Didn't you want to shout as this dragon was once and for all banished from heaven? The seventh trumpet has sounded; God and His Christ have taken their great power and begun to reign. God is moving in, the process has begun, and Satan goes off to make war with the rest of the woman's children who keep the commandments of God and hold to the testimony of Jesus. The day of Jesus' coming is on the way! Watch out, Satan! Watch out all you men who follow him!

Are you ready to unveil more mysteries? Then let's find out more about this beast and what he's up to in Revelation 13.

THE BEAST

Max and Molly are ready to get started on researching the events in Revelation 13. Grab your book and colored pencils, and let's pray for God to give us wisdom and understanding as we study His Word to find out more about the beast in Revelation 13.

Pull out your key-word bookmark. Let's read Revelation 13:1-10 on page 174 and mark the key words listed below on your Observation Worksheets for these ten verses. If you have lost your key-word bookmark, you can turn to page 153 to see how to mark these words:

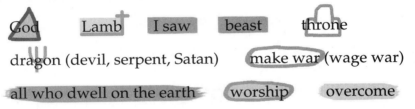

Don't forget to mark your pronouns! And don't forget to double-underline the <u>WHERE</u> in green and mark anything that tells you WHEN with a green clock 🕑 or green circle ◯.

Great! Now let's find out more about this beast by asking the 5 W's and an H questions.

Revelation 13:1 WHERE does this beast come from?

_____

Revelation 13:1-2 WHAT does this beast look like?

_____

_____

_____

WHO gives this beast his power?

_____

Name the three things listed in this verse that the dragon (Satan) gives the beast.

His _____ and his _____ and great

_____.

Revelation 13:3 WHAT do you see about one of the beast's heads?

_____

WHAT happens to this fatal wound?

_____

Revelation 13:3-4 WHOM did the whole earth worship?

_____

Revelation 13:5 HOW long was the beast given to act?

_____

HOW many years is this? _____

Revelation 13:7 WHAT does the beast do?

_____

Revelation 13:8 WHO will worship this beast?

_____

_____

_____

Draw a picture of the beast in the box below.

Now turn back to Revelation 11:7 on page 169. This is the first time we saw this beast.

Revelation 11:7 WHERE does this beast come from?

_____

Revelation 11:3-7 WHOM does the beast kill?

_____

You did an awesome job! Now turn to your time line on page 54 and write "the beast" in the blank under "two witnesses." We know the beast is on the scene at the same time as the two witnesses because he kills them.

Do you have any ideas about WHO this beast might be? You can read more about him in Daniel 7. Scripture describes him in many different ways. Matthew 24:14-15 refers to him as "ABOMINATION OF DESOLATION," 2 Thessalonians 2:3 calls him "the man of lawlessness," and 1 John 2:22 and 1 John 4:3 call him the "antichrist."

Think about all you are learning about him and where his power comes from. As you do your research and gather the facts using other passages of Scripture, you will get a picture of the one God refers to in Genesis 3:15, when He speaks of the enmity between the woman's seed (Jesus) and the serpent's seed. Remember WHO gives the beast his power. This beast is the seed of Satan.

You will learn more about him as we keep studying because this beast plays a key role in the future events on this earth. Remember Revelation 13:9: "If anyone has an ear, let him hear." Keep studying God's Word so that you can recognize this beast that is coming.

Now discover this week's memory verse. Unscramble the words underneath the blanks in the picture of fire and brimstone to complete your verse and find out what happens to those who worship the beast. Then read Revelation 14 to find out the correct verse.

"And the _____ of their _____ goes up
　　　　　　　mokse　　　　　　　　　ortmetn

_____ and _____ ; they have no _____
　　orefevr　　　　　　　vere　　　　　　　　　　　estr

_____ and _____, those who _____
　　ady　　　　　　ignth　　　　　　　　　　orwhisp

the _____ and his _____, and whoever
　　　esabt　　　　　　　　migae

_____ the _____ of his _____."
　　　ecrieves　　　　　　　armk　　　　　　amne

Revelation 14: _____

Great work! Now practice saying this verse out loud three times today.

THE MYSTERY: TWO BEASTS?

"Wow, Max," Molly smiled as she looked at Max's sketch of the beast. "That is a pretty scary-looking beast. Look at the blood oozing from his head!"

Max replied, "That's from his fatal wound."

Miss Kim walked over to take a look. "You're right, Molly. That is one scary and ugly beast! I like the way you have all the people following after him amazed."

"It sure is hard to believe that people would follow a beast like that," Molly said.

"Well, the beast isn't really a beast, and he won't look scary like this. Remember, people will choose to follow him. Keep studying. These descriptions of the beast will show us more about him," said Miss Kim. "Remember we talked about how Scripture describes him as the 'ABOMINATION OF DESOLATION,' 'the man of lawlessness,' and the 'antichrist.' But will those who dwell on the earth see him that way, or will they be deceived? Keep observing. Let's find out what God's Word says."

"All right," Max replied. "I'm ready to go. Let's pray so we can read the rest of Revelation 13 to see what happens next."

Pray, Bible detectives, and then turn to page 176 and read Revelation 13:11-18.

Pull out your key-word bookmark and add the new key words listed below:

another beast (color it orange)

the image of the beast (mark of the beast) (draw a red 666 over it)

Now mark your new key words and the key words listed below on your Observation Worksheet for these verses. But be careful! There is more than one beast in this passage of Scripture!

I saw   beast   signs   worship

those who dwell on the earth

Don't forget to mark your pronouns. And don't forget to double-underline anything that tells you <u>WHERE</u>.

Now let's solve the mystery of this second beast.

Revelation 13:11 WHERE does this second beast come from?

_____

Describe the second beast.

_____

Revelation 13:12 WHAT does this beast do?

_____

_____

Revelation 13:13 WHAT does he perform?

_____

Revelation 13:14 WHAT does he do to those who dwell on the earth?

_____

WHAT does he tell those who dwell on the earth to make?

_____

Revelation 13:15 WHAT did he give to the image of the beast and WHAT could the image do?

He gave _____ to the image of the beast so that the image of the beast could even _____.

WHAT does he cause to happen to those who do not worship the image of the beast?

_____

Revelation 13:15-16 HOW were they to worship the beast?

_____

Revelation 13:17 WHAT happens if you do not have this mark or number of the beast?

_____

Revelation 13:18 WHAT is the number of the beast?

_____

Draw a picture of this event taking place in Revelation 13:13-18.

Did you notice that Satan gives his power to the first beast, but the second beast receives authority from the first beast to perform signs? The second beast even gives the image of the first beast breath so it can speak. That's pretty amazing.

Do you know WHO this second beast is?

____ Yes ____ No

You'll find out as we keep studying.

WHY would those who dwell on the earth worship the beast?

_____

WHO do you think they believe the beast is?

_____

Are they right, or are they deceived? _____

Can you imagine what it would be like to be a Christian in these times? You would not be allowed to buy or sell anything, and you would either have to take the mark and worship the beast or be killed.

Does this sound like Satan, the great dragon, has unleashed his wrath on the earth? It sure does! But one more time, WHO is really in control of all that is happening? ___ ___ ___ It may look like Satan is in control, but you need to remember that God has allowed him to use this power only for a short time. God is still in control over all the events on earth.

Great work! Hang in there and trust God! Don't forget to practice your memory verse!

ANGELS AND THEIR MESSAGES

Today as we head back to the resource room, we are going to get another glimpse of John's vision in heaven. WHAT will we discover? WHAT mystery will these angels reveal? Let's find out by doing our research on Revelation 14. But don't forget to do WHAT? You've got it! Pray!

Now pull out your key-word bookmark and add the new key words listed below:

Babylon (great harlot, woman, great city, mother of harlots) (color it red)

gospel (draw a red megaphone and color it green)

Spirit (draw a purple cloud and color it yellow)

Turn to page 177. Read Revelation 14 and mark your new key words and the key words listed below on your Observation Worksheet:

 God   Jesus (Lamb and any other descriptions of Jesus)

I saw (I looked)   beast   throne   worship

angel   wrath   the image of the beast (mark of the beast)

Don't forget to mark your pronouns! And don't forget to double-underline the <u>WHERE</u> in green and mark anything that tells you WHEN with a green clock 🕐 or green circle ◯.

All right! Tomorrow we'll find out more about these angels flying in midheaven. Don't forget to practice your memory verse!

AN ANGEL WITH THE ETERNAL GOSPEL

Hey, guys, are you ready to find out more about what John saw? Sam is so excited that he is barking and wagging his tail. You know how he loves it when we do our research in the resource room! Why don't you give him his chewy to keep him busy as we discover the events in Revelation 14? Yesterday we marked our key words; today we need to uncover the facts.

Let's pray, then we need to turn to page 177. Read Revelation 14:1-7 and ask the 5 W's and an H.

Revelation 14:1 WHAT does John see?

_____

Let's make a list about these 144,000 to see if they are the same 144,000 we saw in Revelation 7.

144,000

Revelation 14:1 They are with the _____, having his _____ and the _____ of His Father written on their _____.

Revelation 14:3 The 144,000 could learn the new s __ __ __. They have been _____ from the earth.

Revelation 14:4 They have not been _____ with women because they have kept themselves _____. They follow the _____ wherever He goes. They have been purchased from among _____ as _____ _____ to God and to the Lamb.

Revelation 14:5 No _____ was found in their mouth; they are _____.

Do you think that this group of 144,000 is the same group mentioned in Revelation 7? Compare the list you just made with what you learned about the 144,000 in Revelation 7:3-8 (page 160), and in *Bible Prophecy for Kids.* Write out WHY you think they are the same, or WHY you think they aren't on the lines below.

_____

_____

Revelation 14:6 WHAT does John see in this verse?

_____

WHAT does this angel have?

_____

WHO is it going to be preached to?

_____

_____

Does everyone have the opportunity to hear the gospel of Jesus Christ?

_____ Yes _____ No

Look up and read Matthew 24:14. It's a great cross-reference!

WHAT do you learn about the preaching of the gospel?

_____

_____

Turn back to Revelation 14:7. WHAT does this angel say?

_____ God, and give Him _____.

_____ Him who made the _____ and the _____ and _____ and _____ of _____.

WHY are they to fear and worship God? WHAT time is it on earth?

The _____ of His _____ has come.

Do you see how loving and merciful God is? Even with all His judgments on earth, He sends an angel with the eternal gospel. God does not wish for anyone to perish. He is giving mankind another chance to hear the good news of Jesus Christ before it is too late!

Even through all these horrible events on earth, God once again reaches out to man to save him from eternal judgment. One day very soon, Jesus will return to earth, and then it will be too late. They will be without excuse because God will have broadcast His eternal gospel to every nation, tribe, tongue, and people, and their choice will be made.

As you leave today, ask yourself, "Have I made my choice? Have I given my life to Jesus?" If you haven't, then don't wait. You can give your life to Jesus and become a Christian right now.

To become a Christian, the Bible says you need to repent and believe in Jesus. What does it mean to repent? Repent means you change your mind. You need to change your mind about God, Jesus, and you. Do you believe that Jesus is God's Son, that He is God? Jesus was born as a man and lived a perfect life without sin to die and pay for our sins.

WHAT is sin? Sin is to go your own way instead of God's (Isaiah 53:6). Sin is disobeying God; it is doing what God says is wrong. In order to become a Christian, you have to confess. That means you have to agree with God that you are a sinner.

Then you have to believe in Jesus—that He is the Son of God and that He became a human being and died for your sins. If you really mean this and want to become a real Christian, then tell God in your own words. You can write out your prayer to God on the lines below.

Just tell God that you know Jesus died on the cross to pay for your sins, that you are sorry for the things you have done wrong (your sins), and that you want to stop doing things your way and turn your entire life over to Jesus.

_____

_____

_____

_____

If you prayed and asked God to forgive you, then you are now part of God's family! You are God's child, and Jesus and the Holy Spirit will come to live in you (John 14:23).

Now that you have become a part of God's family, you will want to share this great news by telling other people (confessing with your mouth) that you have believed in Jesus Christ and are now a child of God.

If you have already made your choice for Jesus, then ask God to put someone in your life that you can share His gospel with. The gospel is the good news that Jesus came and died to save us from our sins.

Way to go! We are soooooo very proud of you!

MESSAGES OF DOOM AND JUDGMENT

You are doing a fantastic job of unveiling the mysteries in Revelation! Yesterday you saw the 144,000 purchased from the earth with Jesus' and God's names on their foreheads, singing a new song before the throne. Then you saw an angel flying in midheaven with an eternal gospel.

How *exciting* that the God of heaven loves us so much that He doesn't wish for any of us to perish! He keeps sending out His message of love as He continues to judge the earth and those who dwell on it. WHAT messages will these angels reveal today?

Let's find out. Let's pray and turn back to page 177 to Revelation 14. Read Revelation 14:8-20 and ask the 5 W's and an H.

Revelation 14:8 WHAT follows the first angel?

_____

WHAT is this angel's message?

_____

_____

_____

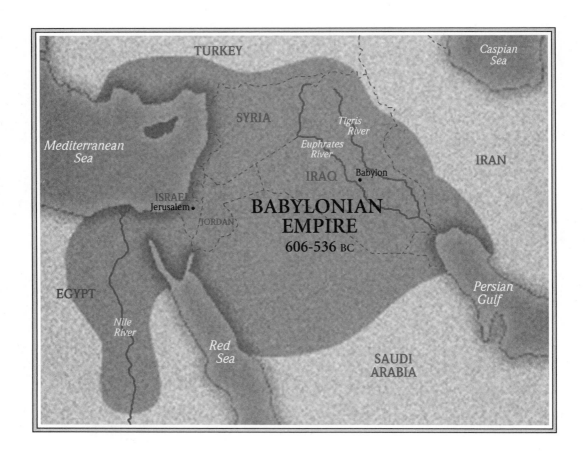

Turn to page 74 to make a list on Babylon. This is a continuing list on Babylon, so only list the things you discover today in Revelation 14. You'll finish the list as you complete your study.

Revelation 14:9-10 WHAT is the third angel's message?

_____

_____

_____

Revelation 14:11 Is there any hope for someone who takes the mark of the beast? _____ HOW long will their torment last?

_____

Revelation 14:12-13 WHAT did we see about those who keep the commandments of God and their faith in Jesus and die in the Lord?

They are b __ __ __ __ __ __, they may r __ __ __ from their labors, their d __ __ __ __ follow with them.

Revelation 14:13 Looking at this verse, do our deeds (the things we do) matter? _____

Revelation 14:14 WHAT does John see?

_____

_____

Revelation 14:15 WHAT does the angel cry out to Him who sat on the cloud?

"Put in your _____ and _____, for the _____ to _____ has come, because the _____ of the _____ is ripe."

Revelation 14:16 WHAT did He do?

_____

Draw a picture of this event in verses 14-16 in the box below.

Revelation 14:17 WHAT do we see about the next angel?

_____

Revelation 14:18 WHAT does the angel mentioned at the beginning of this verse have the power over?

_____

WHAT did this angel call out to the angel with the sickle?

"Put in your _____ _____ and gather the _____ from the _____ of the _____, because her grapes are _____."

Revelation 14:19 WHERE were these clusters thrown?

_____

Revelation 14:20 WHERE was the wine press trodden?

_____

HOW deep and HOW far was the blood?

_____

WHAT does all that you have studied mean? Yesterday we saw the first angel (Revelation 14:6) announce the good news of the gospel. Today we saw the second angel (Revelation 14:8) announce the doom of Babylon, and the third angel (Revelation 14:9-10) announce judgment to those who worship the beast. Then we see John's vision of the earth being reaped with sickles. Two more judgments are coming. A war is on the way.

As the majority of mankind totally rejects God by taking the mark of the beast, God brings forth His great wrath. Revelation 14 gives us the big picture (an overview) of what is on the way in the upcoming chapters. There is a great war coming where the blood will go all the way up to the horse's bridles for a distance of 200 miles. Can you imagine what that war will be like? We'll find out more about this war as we continue unveiling the mysteries of Revelation.

You are doing an awesome job! Don't forget to say your memory verse to a grown-up this week.

WHAT I LEARNED ABOUT **BABYLON**

REVELATION 14:

REVELATION 16:

REVELATION 17:

WHAT I LEARNED ABOUT BABYLON

REVELATION 18:

REVELATION 19:

4

THE SEVEN BOWLS OF WRATH

REVELATION 15–16

You did it! You unveiled another exciting week in Revelation. What do you think about the other beast that has arrived on the scene? Let's call him beast #2. Did you know that beast #2 was the one who would cause those who dwell on the earth to worship the first beast and take his mark or be killed?

And WHAT did you think about those three angels with messages of the gospel, doom, and judgment? Revelation 14 gives us the big picture of some events that are coming.

So WHERE are we on our time line? The last events we added were at the seventh trumpet when the kingdom of the world became the kingdom of our Lord and of His Christ, and Satan was cast down to begin waging his war on earth. WHAT else happens during the sounding of this seventh trumpet? You're about to find out as we continue to unveil the mysteries that God wants us to understand so we will know what is going to happen in the last days.

DAY ONE

ANOTHER SIGN IN HEAVEN

"Hey, Miss Kim, that was a pretty depressing room we went

into this morning," Max said as he, Molly, and Miss Kim headed down the hallway to the resource room.

"Yes, it is," Miss Kim replied. "Just think of how sad it is that people will want to worship the beast's image and proudly wear his mark on their right hand or forehead."

Molly looked at Miss Kim. "That image was pretty scary when we pushed the button and it started speaking."

"I know. As much as we don't like to think about people making that choice, we want the families that visit the museum to have a chance to see what it will be like with the beast on the scene.

"And since it is a little scary, we made sure that kids don't have to go though this room if they don't want to. But the sad thing is, when it actually happens, those who are on the earth won't get that choice. They will have to live with either worshiping the beast or dying for their faith. What a sad day that will be.

"Now that we're back in the resource room, we need to unveil the mystery of the next sign in heaven. Molly, why don't you pray?"

Okay, Bible detectives, now that we have a glimpse of how awful and sad these end times are going to be, let's get back to work on our research. WHAT will we discover in Revelation 15?

Pull out your key-word bookmark and add the new key words listed below:

temple (color it purple)

plagues (bowls) (color it pink)

Turn to page 180. Read Revelation 15 and mark your new key words and the key words listed below on your Observation Worksheet:

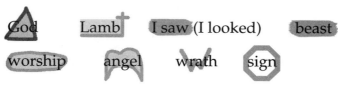

Don't forget to mark your pronouns. And don't forget to double-underline the <u>WHERE</u> in green and mark anything that tells you WHEN with a green clock 🕐 or green circle ⭕.

Now look at the maze below. Find the correct path from Jesus through the clouds, then write the words that you discover on the correct path on the lines below. Check your Observation Worksheet to discover the reference of your verse.

_____

_____

_____

_____

Revelation 16:_____

Way to go! Don't forget to practice this verse. Jesus is coming like a thief. You want to be ready!

SEVEN ANGELS WITH SEVEN PLAGUES

Are you ready to find out more about this sign in heaven? WHAT does John see, and WHAT does it mean? Let's find out. Turn to page 180. Read Revelation 15. Now uncover the mystery. Ask the 5 W's and an H questions to solve the crossword puzzle.

Revelation 15:1 WHAT did John see?

1. (Across) Another _____

WHERE did he see this sign?

2. (Down) In _____

WHAT is this sign? WHAT does John see?

3. (Down) Seven _____ with 4. (Down) _____

5. (Across) _____

WHY are these plagues the last?

6. (Across) Because in them the wrath of _____ is finished.

Revelation 15:2 WHAT did John see on the sea of glass mixed with fire?

7. (Across) Those who have been _____ over the 8. (Down) _____ and his image

WHAT are they holding?

9. (Across) _____ of God

Revelation 15:3 WHAT did they do?

10. (Across) They _____ the song of Moses and

11. (Down) the song of the _____.

Revelation 15:5 WHAT did John see?

12. (Across) The _____ of the tabernacle of testimony in heaven is opened.

Revelation 15:6-7 WHAT came out of the temple, and WHAT did the four living creatures give them?

13. (Across) Seven angels were given seven golden _____ full of the 14. (Across) _____ of God.

Revelation 15:8 WHAT was the temple filled with?

15. (Across) The temple was filled with _____

16. (Down) from the _____ of God

17. (Down) and from His _____.

Revelation 15:8 WHAT do we see about the temple?

18. (Across) No one was able to _____

19. (Down) until the seven plagues were _____.

Great work! Let's pull it together. As we have studied the events of God's judgments on the earth, we saw the Lamb, the only One worthy to open the book, take the seven-sealed book (scroll) and break the seals one at a time. As the seals were broken, we saw seven seal judgments happen on the

earth, including the wrath of God that began in the sixth seal (Revelation 6:16-17).

Then we saw that when the seventh seal was broken, it brought forth seven trumpets and their judgments. From our study today, we see that the seventh trumpet is sounding to bring about seven plagues or bowls, which are the last of God's judgments.

Have you noticed how these judgments have been intensifying, getting worse and worse as they continue? WHAT will happen as we watch these seven angels pour out God's wrath on the earth? We'll find out!

Now don't forget to practice your memory verse. WHAT is Jesus saying to us in this verse? Think about it as you practice saying it out loud three times in a row three times today.

A LOUD VOICE FROM THE TEMPLE

Were you surprised yesterday when you discovered that the sign in heaven was more of God's judgments on the earth? WHAT will happen as these seven angels pour out the bowls of God's wrath? Isn't it amazing that when the seventh bowl is poured out, then the wrath of God is finished? Wow! WHAT will that bring?

There's only one way to find out, and that is to continue our research on the Book of Revelation. Let's head back to the resource room and find out WHAT happens in Revelation 16.

Don't forget to pray! Pull out your key-word bookmark and add the new key words listed below:

Demon(s) (draw a red pitchfork)

I am coming (draw a purple cloud around it and color it in three parts: the first part blue, the middle part yellow, and the last part blue)

false prophet (color it orange)

Turn to page 182. Read Revelation 16 and mark your new key words and the key words listed below on your Observation Worksheet:

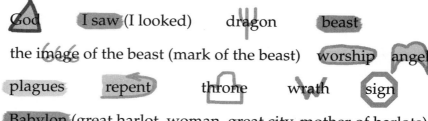

God   I saw (I looked)   dragon   beast

the image of the beast (mark of the beast)   worship   angel

plagues   repent   throne   wrath   sign

Babylon (great harlot, woman, great city, mother of harlots)

Don't forget to mark your pronouns. And don't forget to double-underline the <u>WHERE</u> in green and mark anything that tells you WHEN with a green clock ⏲ or green circle◯.

Way to go! Don't forget to practice your memory verse.

FIVE ANGELS WITH FIVE PLAGUES

Your research is really coming along. Just look at all you have discovered by simply studying God's Word. Today we need to head back to Revelation 16 and find out WHAT happens as five angels pour out God's plagues. WHOM will these plagues affect? The trumpet judgments destroyed a third of the earth, sea, rivers, and springs. Also, a third of the sun, moon, and stars were darkened. Then three woes of the last

three trumpets brought about locusts who tormented but could
not kill, and armies of horses who killed a third of mankind,
while the kingdom of this world became the kingdom of our
Lord and His Christ.

A third of this earth and a third of mankind has been
destroyed. WHAT will God strike next? Let's find out. Turn to
page 182. Pray and then read Revelation 16:1-11. Answer the 5
W's and an H questions.

Revelation 16:1 WHAT did John hear?

_____

WHERE did this loud voice come from?

_____

WHAT did this loud voice tell the seven angels to do?

_____

_____

Revelation 16:2 WHAT happened when the first angel
poured his bowl on the earth?

A loathsome and _____ _____
appeared on the people who had the _____ of the
_____ and who _____ his _____.

Look at Revelation 16:2 and underline the word *first* in pink
and write a *1* beside this verse to show this is the first bowl.

Turn to page 92 and draw a picture of this first bowl on the
chart for the seven bowls.

Revelation 16:3 WHAT happened when the second angel
poured his bowl into the sea?

The sea became _____ and _____ _____
thing in the _____ _____.

Wow! HOW much was affected? Is it a third like it was in
the trumpet judgment? ____ Yes ____ No
HOW much? _____
Are the judgments getting worse? _____

Underline the word *second* in pink and write a 2 beside this
verse to show this is the second bowl.
Turn to page 92 and draw a picture of this second bowl on
the chart for the seven bowls.

Revelation 16:4 WHAT happened when the third angel
poured his bowl into the rivers and the springs of
water?

They became _____.

Revelation 16:6 WHY did God give them blood to
drink?

_____

_____

WHAT did the angel say about the judgment?

"They _____ it."

Revelation 16:7 WHAT do you see about God's judgments?

_____

Underline the word *third* in pink and write a 3 beside this
verse to show this is the third bowl.
Turn to page 92 and draw a picture of this third bowl on the
chart for the seven bowls.

Revelation 16:8-9 WHAT happened when the fourth angel poured his bowl upon the sun?

The sun _____ men with _____. They were scorched with fierce _____.

Did these men turn to God? _____ HOW did they react to this plague?

They _____ the _____ of God. They did not _____ so as to give God _____.

WHAT do you see about God?

He has the _____ over these _____.

Underline the word *fourth* in pink and write a 4 beside this verse to show this is the fourth bowl.
Turn to page 92 and draw a picture of this fourth bowl on the chart for the seven bowls.

Revelation 16:10 WHAT happened when the fifth angel poured his bowl on the throne of the beast?

The beast's _____ became _____, and they _____ their _____ because of _____.

Revelation 16:11 HOW did they react to this judgment?

They _____ the _____ of heaven and did not _____ of their _____.

Underline the word *fifth* in pink and write a 5 beside this verse to show this is the fifth bowl.
Turn to page 92 and draw a picture of this fifth bowl on the chart for the seven bowls.
Great artwork! Drawing these pictures will help you remember these bowls of wrath that are poured on the earth.

Don't forget to practice your memory verse. Tomorrow we will watch as the last two angels pour out their bowls. Keep up the good work!

IT IS DONE!

"Hey, Max, come over here. How do you like my sketch of the angel pouring out the plague on those who took the mark of the beast?"

"Those are some pretty ugly sores, Molly," Max said as he looked over her drawing. "And you were talking about how ugly and gross my beast was. This is just as bad."

"Yeah, it is, but the Bible did say it was a loathsome and malignant sore. That means it has to be pretty ugly."

"I bet it really hurts too," Max replied. "Let's get back to our research so we can find out what the next plagues are."

"I'm ready if you are! You read first."

Okay, Bible detectives, let's do our research. Don't forget to pray. Turn to page 183. Read Revelation 16:12-21. Unveil God's Word by asking the 5 W's and an H.

Revelation 16:12 WHAT happened when the sixth angel poured his bowl on the great river, the Euphrates?

_____

WHAT is the importance of the drying up of the Euphrates?

So that the _____ would be _____ for the _____ from the _____.

Underline the word *sixth* in pink and write a 6 beside this verse to show this is the sixth bowl.

Turn to page 92 and draw a picture of this sixth bowl on the chart for the seven bowls.

Revelation 16:13 WHO are the three that John sees?

_____

This shows you WHO the second beast is that you marked in Revelation 13:11. WHO is this other beast (beast #2)? WHAT is he called in Revelation 16:13?

_____

Revelation 16:13-14 WHAT are these three up to?

Three unclean _____ like _____ came out

of their _____, spirits of _____, performing
_____ to gather the _____ together for the _____
of the great day of _____.

Did you notice that the dragon, Satan, has an unholy trinity of the dragon, the beast, and the false prophet that imitates God's holy trinity of God, Jesus, and the Holy Spirit?

This drying of the great river and these unholy three (dragon, beast, and false prophet) are gathering the kings for the war we saw would be coming in Revelation 14.

Revelation 16:15 WHAT do we see about Jesus?

_____

WHAT are we to do? HOW are we blessed?

_____

Are you doing that? Are you staying awake (keeping watch)? Are you on the alert, ready for Jesus' coming? Are you being faithful by doing what God wants you to do? _____

Revelation 16:16 WHERE is the war going to be? WHERE are they gathered?

_____

Revelation 16:17 WHAT happened when the seventh angel poured his bowl upon the air?

A loud _____ came out of the _____ from the throne and said, " _____ _____ _____."

Underline the word *seventh* in pink and write a 7 beside this verse to show this is the seventh bowl.

Turn to page 92 and draw a picture of this seventh bowl on the chart for the seven bowls.

Revelation 16:18 WHAT happens as this last bowl is poured out?

There were flashes of _____ and sounds and peals of _____ and a _____ _____.

Have you seen this happen before? Look back at Revelation 8:1-5.

WHAT had been broken? _____

Look at Revelation 11:15-19.

WHAT had been sounded? _____

Isn't this amazing how God brings about lightning, thunder, and an earthquake after the last of the seventh seal, seventh trumpet, and seventh bowl?

Revelation 16:19-21 WHAT happened because of this earthquake?

The great city was _____ into _____ _____.

The cities of the _____ _____.

Babylon the great was _____ before God and given the cup of His _____ _____.

Every _____ fled away and the _____ were not found.

Huge _____ about _____ pounds each came down from heaven upon _____.

WHAT did these men do?

They _____ God.

Turn to page 74. Add what you learned about Babylon in Revelation 16:19 to your chart.

Looking at WHAT you saw about Babylon, WHEN did she fall? During WHAT judgment? _____

If you aren't sure, look back a few verses at Revelation 16:17 to help you see WHEN this is happening.

WHAT is done, now that the seventh bowl has been poured out?

Look at Revelation 15:1. WHAT is finished?

_____

Great work! Now turn to your time line on page 54 and find this bowl and write out when Babylon fell and when the wrath of God is finished based on what you discovered today.

Way to go! You have done an awesome job! Now don't forget to say your memory verse to a grown-up.

THE SEVEN BOWL JUDGMENTS	
1ˢᵗ Bowl	**2ⁿᵈ Bowl**
A _____ on those with the _____	_____ became _____ Everything in _____ died
3ʳᵈ Bowl	**4ᵗʰ Bowl**
_____ & _____ became _____	Men were _____ with fierce _____
5ᵗʰ Bowl	**6ᵗʰ Bowl**
_____ of beast d _ _ _ _ _ ed	_____ dried up
7ᵗʰ Bowl	
Poured out upon the _____—God's _____ is finished.	

5

THE MYSTERY OF BABYLON

REVELATION 17–18

How did you like the room in the museum with the angels and the seven plagues? Pretty cool, huh, getting to add red food coloring to the "seas" and putting those floating fish in to mimic the death of every living thing in the seas? Those moans and groans of the people in the beast's kingdom were a little unnerving. This museum is such an awesome place!

WHAT will we discover this week? We are going to uncover the mystery of Babylon the great. Are you ready to uncover WHY God would give her the cup of His fierce wrath? Let's head back to the resource room and find out.

DAY ONE

UNVEILING THE MYSTERY

Hey, guys, come on in. We're just getting out our colored pencils so we can start our research. Why don't you pray, and then we'll be ready to get to work? Let's turn to page 185. Read Revelation 17. Then pull out your key-word bookmark and mark the following key words:

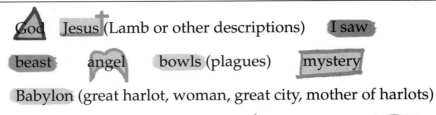

God   Jesus (Lamb or other descriptions)   I saw

beast   angel   bowls (plagues)   mystery

Babylon (great harlot, woman, great city, mother of harlots)

those who dwell on the earth   kings (kingdom)   wage war

Don't forget to mark your pronouns! And don't forget to double-underline the <u>WHERE</u> in green and mark anything that tells you WHEN with a green clock or a green circle.

Now let's discover your memory verse by connecting the dots in the puzzle below. Start at number 1 and connect all the dots. Then go back and write the word that goes with each dot on the lines underneath the puzzle and unveil the mystery of the woman. Finally, look at Revelation 17 to discover the reference for this verse.

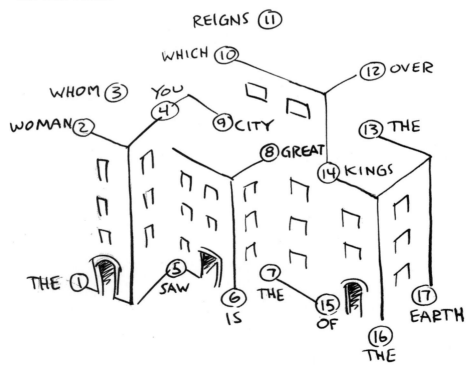

"_____ _____ _____ _____ _____ _____
   1   2   3   4   5   6

_____ _____ _____, _____ _____ _____
   7   8   9   10   11   12

_____ _____ _____ _____ _____."
 13   14   15   16   17

Revelation 17:_____

You did it! Don't forget to practice saying your verse!

THE TEN HORNS OF THE BEAST

Good morning! It's great to have you back! Are you ready to discover more about this beast you have been studying? Today as you study Revelation 17, you are going to uncover the meaning of the seven heads and the ten horns of the beast. Doesn't that sound interesting?

But before you get started, WHAT do you need to do first? You remembered! Pray! There is no way we could ever unveil these mysteries without God's Spirit leading and guiding us as we study Scripture.

Turn to page 185 and read Revelation 17. Solve the mystery. Ask those 5 W's and an H.

Revelation 17:3 HOW is the beast described?

_____

_____

Revelation 17:7 WHOM does the beast carry?

_____

Revelation 17:8 WHERE is the beast coming out of?

_____

WHERE is he going?

_____

WHAT do we learn about those who dwell on the earth?

_____

Revelation 17:9 WHAT are the seven heads of the beast?

_____

Revelation 17:10 WHAT are these seven mountains?

_____

WHAT do we learn about these kings?

_____ have fallen, _____ is, the other has _____

_____ _____.

Revelation 17:11 WHAT else do we learn about the beast?

_____

Revelation 17:12 WHAT are the ten horns?

_____

WHAT do the ten horns receive?

_____

Revelation 17:14 HOW do the beast and these ten horns relate to the Lamb?

_____

WHAT does the Lamb do to them?

_____

WHAT do you learn about the Lamb? HOW is he described?

_____

WHO are those with the Lamb?

_____

Revelation 17:15 WHAT are the waters where the harlot sits?

_____

Revelation 17:16 WHAT do the ten horns and the beast do to the harlot?

_____

_____

Revelation 17:17 WHAT do the ten horns give the beast?

_____

WHY do they do this?

_____

So WHO is in control? _____

Isn't this awesome? The beast will have power, but only

because God uses it to execute His purpose. Everything that happens is because God wills it. He is the One in control—not the beast, not the kings, and not the dragon. WHO wins the war? The Lamb! And if you are His, if you have believed in Jesus like we talked about, then you are the chosen and the faithful and you will be with Him! We have nothing to fear because we know WHO is in control and WHO wins!

All right! Tomorrow we will find out more about this mystery woman.

WHO IS THIS WOMAN?

Yesterday was awesome as we saw that God is still in control, even with this powerful beast on the loose. Isn't it amazing how God uses this beast for His plans and purposes?

Today we're going to take a closer look at the woman we unveiled in our memory verse. WHO is this woman, and WHY is God going to pour out His fierce wrath on her? Let's find out by turning to page 185 and reading Revelation 17.

Now look at your Observation Worksheets at every place where you marked *Babylon, the great harlot, woman, great city,* and *mother of harlots.* Uncover the mystery of this woman by turning to page 74 and writing what you learn about this woman from Revelation 17 on your chart on Babylon.

Great work! Now think about all you have learned about Babylon from Revelation 14–17.

Revelation 17:18 WHO did you discover this woman is?

_____

Revelation 17:16 WHAT will happen to this woman (this city)?

_____

_____

Do you know WHERE this city is mentioned the first time in the Bible? Let's find out.

Look up and read Genesis 11:4.

WHAT did they want to build for themselves?

_____

WHAT did they want to make for themselves?

_____

Genesis 11:6-8 WHAT did God think about this? Did He want them to make a name for themselves, or did He want them to follow Him?

_____

WHAT did God do so they would stop building this city?

_____

Genesis 11:9 WHAT is the name of this city?

_____

Does the name Babel sound familiar? This city called Babel is Babylon. From the days of Genesis, this city has been in opposition to God. They wanted to make a name for themselves instead of having God rule over them. That is sin!

As we continue our study in Revelation 18, we will find out

more about Babylon's destruction, which happens because of Babylon's rebellion.

Keep up the good work! Don't forget to practice your memory verse.

BABYLON HAS FALLEN!

Miss Kim walked into the resource room and greeted Molly and Max. "I just saw your Uncle Jake in the hallway, and he told me he had taken you into the Babylon room. How did you like the idea of being able to knock down the city?"

"We thought it was cool!" Molly smiled at Miss Kim. "Max let Sam loose, and 'you know who' knocked the city down before we had a chance to do anything else."

Miss Kim laughed. "Are you ready to find out more about what happens to this city, and how the people feel about its destruction?"

"Yes! Let's get back to work."

Okay, pull out your key-word bookmark and add the new key word listed below:

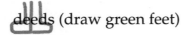 deeds (draw green feet)

Turn to page 187. Read Revelation 18 and mark your new key word and the key words listed below on your Observation Worksheet:

 God   I saw   angel   demons   kings

 Babylon (great harlot, woman, great city, mother of harlots)

woe

Don't forget to mark your pronouns! And don't forget to double-underline the <u>WHERE</u> in green and mark anything that tells you WHEN with a green clock ⏰ or green circle ◯ .

Keep an eye out for the time phrases *one hour* and *one day*, and make sure you mark them with a green clock.

Way to go! You did great! Now practice saying your memory verse.

JUDGMENT HAS COME!

You did a wonderful job observing Revelation 18 yesterday. Are you ready to find out WHO will mourn over this city's destruction, while other people rejoice? WHY is there rejoicing? Let's find out. Pray and turn to page 187. Read Revelation 18.

Now ask the 5 W's and an H.

Revelation 18:1-2 WHAT does this angel have to say about Babylon?

"_____ , _____ is Babylon the _____!"

Turn to page 187 and look at every place you marked *Babylon* on your Observation Worksheet. List everything you see about this city in Revelation 18 on your chart on page 75.

Revelation 18:10 WHEN does her judgment come?

_____

Now that Babylon has fallen, do you remember seeing that this was coming in Revelation 14:8?

WHEN does Babylon fall? WHERE did you place this event

on your time line? Do you remember? Look at your time line on page 54 if you don't remember.

Revelation 18:11-17 HOW do the different groups of people mentioned in these verses respond to Babylon's destruction?

_____

Revelation 18:20 WHO were to rejoice?

_____

WHY?

_____

Wow! Are you amazed at how God fulfills His Word and brings about His perfect plan? You have seen that throughout history Babylon has chosen to go against God, but in one hour you see God judge her and burn her up with fire. God has begun to reign!

Did you know that the city of Babylon is being rebuilt in Iraq?

Could this be the "Babylon" of Revelation that will be destroyed in one hour, in one day? Only time will reveal if this is the same Babylon. You may not know all the details, but you know what is coming. You have been faithful to study God's Word. You know a war is coming, and the Lamb will overcome!

6

jESUS iS COMiNG!

REVELATION 19–20

Don't those words "Jesus is coming" excite you? This week we are finally going to see Jesus' return to the earth. WHAT will happen when the Lamb returns? Remember, we saw a war was coming in Revelation 14, with blood up to the horses' bridles for a distance of 200 miles! This is going to be one action-packed week. So grab those Bibles and head back to the museum. Jesus is coming, and we don't want to miss a moment of this important event!

DAY ONE

HALLELUJAH! THE LORD REIGNS

It's great to have you back this week! Are you ready to stand up and shout, "Hallelujah" and praises to the Lord our God, who has brought about all these things so that we can rule and reign with Him?

Why don't you take a moment to thank God for all that He has revealed to you as you have studied this awesome book? He is such a good God, who shares His plans of what He is about to do.

Now pull out your key-word bookmark and add the new key word listed below:

bride (box it in purple)

Turn to page 191. Read Revelation 19:1-10 and mark your new key word and the key words listed below on your Observation Worksheet:

 God   Jesus (Lamb)   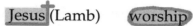 worship   throne

Babylon (great harlot, woman, great city, mother of harlots)

Don't forget to mark your pronouns! And don't forget to double-underline the <u>WHERE</u> in green and mark anything that tells you WHEN with a green clock 🕐 or green circle ◯ .

Now solve the mystery. Ask the 5 W's and an H to discover WHAT event is taking place.

Revelation 19:1 WHAT did John hear in heaven?

_____

Revelation 19:1-2 WHAT did this multitude say?

"_____! _____ and _____ and
_____ belong to our _____; because His
_____ are _____ and _____."

Revelation 19:2 WHY did they say this about God?

_____

Turn to page 75 and add these last things you see about Babylon from Revelation 19 to your list.

Revelation 19:4-6 WHAT is happening in these verses?

_____

Draw a picture in the box below that shows WHAT is happening in Revelation 19:1-6.

Now read Revelation 19:6b-10.

Revelation 19:7 WHAT event is taking place?

_____

Revelation 19:8 WHAT was the bride clothed in?

_____

WHAT is this fine linen?

_____

Revelation 19:9 WHO are blessed?

_____

Do you know WHO this bride is? The bride is the church of Jesus Christ. Anyone who accepts Jesus Christ as his or her Savior becomes a part of Christ's church, who is His bride.

Ephesians 5:23-32 gives a picture of our relationship with Christ as that of a marriage relationship between a husband (Christ) and a wife (the church).

Draw a picture of this event in Revelation 19:6b-10 in the box below.

Outstanding artwork! Aren't you excited to know that if you have accepted Jesus Christ as your Savior, you are His bride? We won't just attend the marriage supper of the Lamb. We will be part of it! Keep those garments. You are clothing yourself in righteousness if you are keeping your garments (doing the things that God shows you in His Word) so that you will be prepared for His coming as a bride is prepared for her bridegroom.

Now let's head out and solve the mystery of this week's memory verse. To solve this mystery, you need to decide which of the missing vowels (a, e, i, o, u) needs to go on each of the blanks. Once you have added the vowels to the blanks and unveiled your verse, find the reference that goes with this verse.

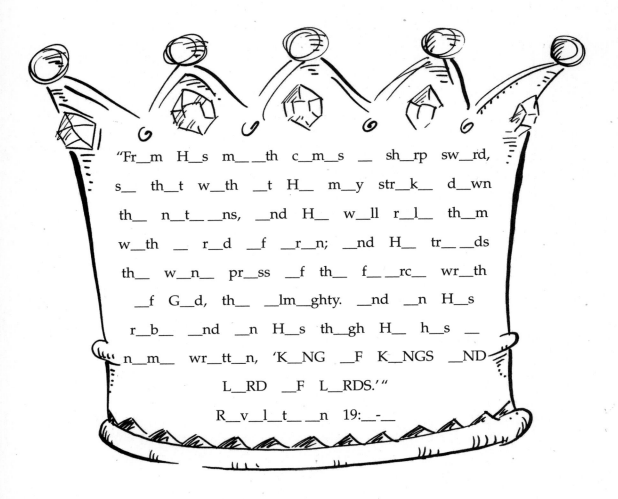

"Fr__m H__s m____th c__m__s __ sh__rp sw__rd, s__ th__t w__th __t H__ m__y str__k__ d__wn th__ n__t____ns, __nd H__ w__ll r__l__ th__m w__th __ r__d __f __r__n; __nd H__ tr____ds th__ w__n__ pr__ss __f th__ f____rc__ wr__th __f G__d, th__ __lm__ghty. __nd __n H__s r__b__ __nd __n H__s th__gh H__ h__s __ n__m__ wr__tt__n, 'K__NG __F K__NGS __ND L__RD __F L__RDS.'"

R__v__l__t____n 19:__-__

All right! Way to go! Now don't forget to practice saying this verse three times today to remind you that the King of kings and Lord of lords is on His way!

kiNG OF kiNGS
AND LORD OF LORDS!

Molly and Max walked into the resource room. "Today's the big day, Miss Kim."

"It sure is, Max! Are you ready?"

"I am. Once we do our research, will we get to see this event in the museum?"

"Yes. Since this is such an amazing event, we have a very special video to play on the IMAX screen to make you feel like you are really there."

Molly squealed. "That sounds like so much fun. Let's get started on our research so that we can know what to expect."

Are you ready, Bible detectives? Grab those colored pencils and let's do our research. Turn to page 193. Read Revelation 19:11-16. Pull out your key-word bookmark and mark the following key words:

 God   Jesus (or any description that refers to Jesus)

 I saw   wages war   wrath

Don't forget to mark your pronouns!

Now answer the 5 W's and an H to create your master-pieces!

Revelation 19:11 WHAT did John see?

_____

_____

WHAT does He do?

In _____ He _____ and _____
_____

WHAT is the One who sits on the horse called?

_____

Revelation 19:12-13 HOW is He described?

"His eyes are a _____ of _____, and on His
head are many _____; and He has a _____
written on Him which no one _____ except Himself.

He is clothed with a _____ dipped in _____ and His name is called The _____ of _____."

Does this description sound familiar? Have you seen this in Revelation 1? WHO is this? _____

Revelation 19:14 WHO is with Him?

_____

WHAT are they wearing?

_____

Is this the same group of people we saw in Revelation 19:7-8?

_____ Yes _____ No

Revelation 19:15 WHAT comes out of His mouth, and WHAT does He do with it?

_____

WHAT will He do with the nations?

_____

WHAT does He tread?

_____

Revelation 19:16 WHAT name is written on His robe and His thigh?

_____

Doesn't this name just make you want to shout? Is this the event that Christians have been looking forward to since Jesus left to prepare a place for us in heaven (John 14:2)?

Draw a picture of this awesome event in Revelation 19:11-16 in the box below.

Now, turn to page 54 and put Jesus' second coming in the cloud on your time line. You know this event happens after the seventh bowl is poured on the air and Babylon is destroyed.

Wow! Wasn't it exciting seeing Jesus on that white horse? This is not the same white horse that we saw in Revelation 6. Remember, in Revelation 6, Jesus is the Lamb in heaven that is breaking the seals. The rider of Revelation 6 comes from the seal being broken. WHO do you think the rider of Revelation 6 is?

_____

Did you notice WHAT was on Jesus' thigh? Most warriors ride into battle with their swords on their thighs. WHERE is Jesus' sword? It will come out of His mouth. Isn't that awesome?

What an exciting day! Jesus is our conquering King! He is about to set up His earthly kingdom. Say that memory verse and get excited as you say His name!

THE BATTLE OF HAR-MAGEDON

"Hey," Max called out to Molly, "do you want to use the watercolors as we work on our artwork today?"

"That sounds like a great idea. I'll fill some cups up with water. You bring the paints and paper."

"All set. I'll pray, and then we can get to work."

Pull out your key-word bookmark, Bible detectives, and add the new key word listed below:

lake of fire (draw and color it like fire)

Now turn to page 193. Read Revelation 19:17-21 and mark your new key word and the key words listed below on your Observation Worksheet:

God   Jesus   angel   beast   make war

the image of the beast   false prophet   worship

Don't forget to mark your pronouns!

Now get the facts. Ask those 5 W's and an H.

Revelation 19:17 WHAT does this angel say to the birds that fly in midheaven?

"_____, assemble for the great _____ of _____."

Revelation 19:18 WHAT are these birds going to eat?

_____

_____

Draw a picture of this event in Revelation 19:17-18 in the box below.

```
┌─────────────────────────────────────────────────────┐
│                                                       │
│                                                       │
│                                                       │
│                                                       │
│                                                       │
│                                                       │
│                                                       │
│                                                       │
│                                                       │
│                                                       │
│                                                       │
│                                                       │
│                                                       │
│                                                       │
└─────────────────────────────────────────────────────┘
```

Read Revelation 19:19-21.

Revelation 19:19 WHAT did John see?

The _____ and the _____ of the earth and their _____ assembled to _____ _____ against _____ who sat on the _____ and against _____ _____.

Is this the war we have been reading about? _____

Revelation 19:20 WHAT happened to the beast and the false prophet?

_____

Revelation 19:21 WHAT happened to the rest?

_____

Draw a picture of this event in Revelation 19:19-21 in the box below.

Were you surprised when the loud voice told the birds to assemble so they could eat the flesh of those warring against the Lamb? Will anyone escape in this battle against the King of kings? No way! They will fall by the sword, and the birds are going to eat their flesh on this great day. The only ones to escape are the beast and the false prophet, which isn't really an escape since they are thrown into the lake of fire forever and ever.

SATAN IS BOUND!

"What can I say? That was the most amazing video I have ever seen," Max said as they walked out of the IMAX theater. "How did you like it, Molly?"

"That was a lot of blood—a really, really, really lot of blood!"

Miss Kim, Uncle Jake, and Max burst out laughing. Jake smiled and winked at Max. "I bet your favorite part was those birds."

"Yuck! No way! It is so hard to believe that there is going to be such an awful war. I did like the part with the armies in their white linen, with all that blood and not one speck of it ended up on the armies."

"That's because the armies didn't fight. Jesus defeated the kings and their armies with the sword out of His mouth," Jake reminded him.

Max looked at Miss Kim. "Thank you for letting us help you get the museum ready. It has been a fantastic experience. I will never forget it."

"You're welcome, Max. You have helped us out too. By trying out our experiments, we know what works and what we might do a little differently. You and Molly have worked hard and made this so much fun." Sam jumped up and barked at Miss Kim. "Well, Sam," Miss Kim said as she scratched his head, "you have definitely made this an interesting adventure!" Everyone cracked up laughing as Sam started jumping and running in excited circles around Miss Kim.

Okay, guys, we are back at the resource room. We need to pray and get back to work so we can find out WHAT happens next. The beast and false prophet are in the lake of fire. WHERE is the dragon?

Pull out your key-word bookmark and add the new key words listed below:

the dead (color it black)

first resurrection (circle it in green and color it pink)

Now turn to page 194. Read Revelation 20:1-6 and mark your new key words and the key words listed below on your Observation Worksheet:

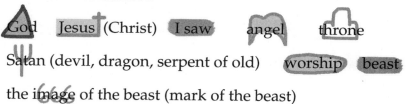

God   Jesus (Christ)   I saw   angel   throne

Satan (devil, dragon, serpent of old)   worship   beast

the image of the beast (mark of the beast)

Don't forget to mark your pronouns! And don't forget to double-underline the <u>WHERE</u> in green and mark anything that tells you WHEN with a green clock 🕐 or green circle ◯.

Revelation 20:1 WHAT did the angel have in his hand?

_____

Revelation 20:2 WHAT did the angel do?

_____

Revelation 20:3 WHY did the angel do this?

_____

HOW long would he be bound?

_____

Draw a picture of this event in Revelation 20:1-3.

Revelation 20:4 WHAT did John see?

_____

WHO are these souls?

_____

_____

WHAT happened to them?

They came to _____ and _____ with _____
for a _____ _____.

Revelation 20:5-6 WHAT is this called?

_____

Draw a picture of this event in Revelation 20:4-6.

[blank drawing box]

Now turn back to page 54. On your time line add "Satan bound" and "Christ's 1,000-year reign." You know that these two events happen after Jesus returns.

These are two very important events. Can you imagine an earth without Satan? That's a pretty amazing event. WHAT will happen after 1,000 years? We'll find out. Keep up the good work!

THE GREAT WHITE THRONE JUDGMENT

Wasn't it exciting to watch the angel coming down out of heaven with a chain and a key to the abyss? Did you know he was going to bind Satan and put him in a bottomless pit for a thousand years? There will be a thousand years of peace with Christ reigning on earth. Can you imagine living in peace? That means no wars and no sad stories of killing for a thousand years. WHAT an awesome time that will be!

WHAT will happen once those thousand years are over? Do you know? Let's find out. Pull out your key-word bookmark, Bible detectives, and add the new key words listed below:

second death (underline it twice in black)

according to their deeds (according to what he has done) (circle it in green and color it green)

Turn to page 195. Read Revelation 20:7-15 and mark your new key words and the key words listed below on your Observation Worksheet:

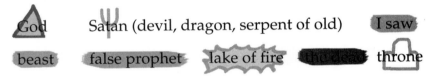

God   Satan (devil, dragon, serpent of old)   I saw

beast   false prophet   lake of fire   the dead   throne

Don't forget to mark your pronouns! And don't forget to double-underline the WHERE in green and mark anything that tells you WHEN with a green clock 🕐 or green circle ⭕.

Revelation 20:7 WHAT will happen when the thousand years are complete?

_____

Revelation 20:8-9 WHAT will he do?

He will _____ out to _____ the _____ and _____ them together for the _____.

Revelation 20:9 WHAT did they surround?

_____

WHAT happened to them?

_____

Revelation 20:10 WHAT happened to the devil?

_____

HOW long will they be tormented?

_____

Draw a picture of this event in Revelation 20:7-10.

Read Revelation 20:11-15.

Revelation 20:11 WHAT did John see?

_____

WHAT happens to the heaven and earth?

_____

Revelation 20:12 WHO were before the throne?

_____

Do you know WHO "the dead" are? The dead are those who have rejected Jesus Christ. They never accepted Him as their Lord and Savior.

WHAT was opened?

_____

HOW were the dead judged?

_____

Revelation 20:14 WHAT happened to death and Hades?

_____

WHAT is the second death?

_____

Revelation 20:15 WHO are thrown into the lake of fire?

_____

Draw a picture to show the great white throne judgment in Revelation 20:11-15.

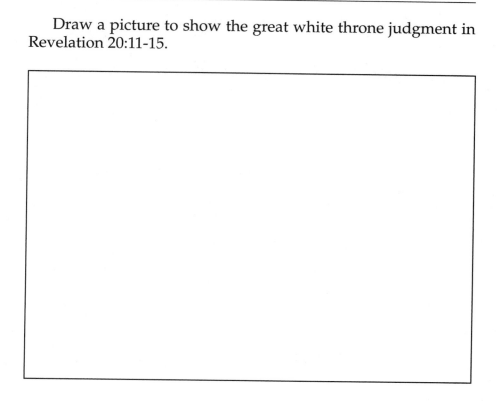

Now turn to your time line on page 54, and put this great white throne judgment on your time line after Christ's 1,000-year reign.

Will everyone who goes into the lake of fire suffer the same degree of punishment? No. We see very plainly that all of these people standing around are going to the lake of fire, but some will have a punishment worse than others.

Some of these people were nice people; they did good things while they were on earth. But it isn't being good that gets us into heaven. The only way into heaven is by believing in and accepting Jesus Christ as our Savior (John 14:6). It's giving our lives over to Him.

Just think: All of these people standing around are going to the lake of fire because they refused to believe in Jesus. They will spend eternity in the lake of fire, but how bad their punishment will be depends on how they lived on earth. They will be judged by their deeds, by how much truth they had, and by what they did with that truth. What a very sad day that will be—to be doomed to eternity in the lake of fire burning with brimstone all because they rejected the One who created and died for them!

God gives each and every one of us a choice. We can choose to live for Him and spend eternity in heaven, or we can choose to follow Satan and spend eternity with him, the beast, and the false prophet in the lake of fire and brimstone.

Don't forget to say your verse this week to a grown-up. Never forget that the King is coming and then the judgment.

7

THE NEW JERUSALEM

REVELATION 21–22

Can you believe it? This is our last week in Revelation! Studying Revelation has been such an awesome experience. We are so glad that you have hung in there and persevered until the end.

Perseverance is such an important quality to have. It means we don't give up. We don't walk away just because something is hard and difficult. We finish what we start. We hang in there until the very end! You have done that, and just look at all you have discovered. You know what is going to happen in the future! Isn't that wonderful?

Last week we saw some incredible events: the marriage of the bride and the Lamb, Jesus' out-of-this-world second coming, a war with more blood and death than you can imagine, the beast and false prophet being thrown into the lake of fire, Satan being bound, and Jesus' 1,000-year reign. Then Satan is loosed, deceives the nations, and is sent to the lake of fire forever, as the great white throne judgment takes place and those who haven't accepted Jesus and whose names aren't in the book of life are thrown into the lake of fire and brimstone. Whew! What a week!

This week is a very special week that belongs to those who have believed in Jesus Christ and given their lives to Him. We are going to see WHAT it's going to be like in eternity. WHAT will heaven be like? Let's find out.

A NEW HEAVEN
AND A NEW EARTH

You're back! We are so excited! As soon as we finish our research, we get to step back into the "heaven" room at the museum. We can't wait! So let's get to work. Pull out your key-word bookmark, Bible detectives, and add the new key word listed below:

holy city (New Jerusalem, the city) (color it purple)

Turn to page 197. Read Revelation 21:1-8 and mark your new key word and the key words listed below on your Observation Worksheet:

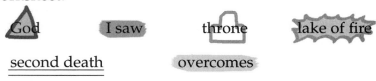

second death   overcomes

Don't forget to mark your pronouns! Mark anything that tells you WHEN by drawing a green clock like this: 🕐 or green circle ◯ .

Revelation 21:1 WHAT did John see?

_____

WHAT happened to the first heaven and earth?

_____

WHAT is no longer there? _____

Revelation 21:2 WHAT came down out of heaven?

_____

Revelation 21:3 WHAT is now among men?

_____

Revelation 21:3-4 WHAT will God do?

He will _____ among them. They will be His _____, and He will _____ away every _____ from their _____.

Revelation 21:5 WHAT is God doing?

_____

Revelation 21:6 WHAT did God say?

_____

WHAT do we see about God?

_____

WHAT will God give those who thirst?

_____

Revelation 21:7 WHO will inherit these things?

_____

Do you remember all the cool things the overcomer receives from your study in *Bible Prophecy for Kids?* If you don't, check out Revelation 2–3 and look for the verses where Jesus says this key phrase: "to him who overcomes." Look at each promise Jesus gives the overcomer, or pull out your *Bible Prophecy for Kids* book and look at your chart on page 91.

Revelation 21:8 WHO will be in the lake of fire?

_____

_____

_____

Now solve your last memory verse. Take a look at the high wall that surrounds the new Jerusalem on page 129. As you look at this awesome sight, you need to look at the passages of Scripture listed below to find out WHAT won't be in heaven and list those things next to each Scripture reference.

Turn to page 197 and read the passages listed below in Revelation 21–22.

WHAT won't be in the new Jerusalem?

Revelation 21:4 No longer will there be any _____, _____, or _____, or _____.

Revelation 21:8 But for the _____ and _____ and _____ and _____ and _____ persons and _____ and _____ and all _____, their part will be in the lake of fire.

Revelation 21:22 There will be no _____ in it.

Revelation 21:23 The city has no need of the _____ or of the _____ to shine.

Revelation 21:25 There will be no _____there, and its gates never _____.

Revelation 21:27 Nothing _____, and no one who practices _____ and _____, shall ever come into it.

Revelation 22:3 There will no longer be any _____.

Now look at the words inscribed in the wall below and put an X over each word in the wall if it *won't* be in the new Jerusalem.

Then take the words that are left in the wall and place them in order on the blanks on page 130 to discover Jesus' message to us.

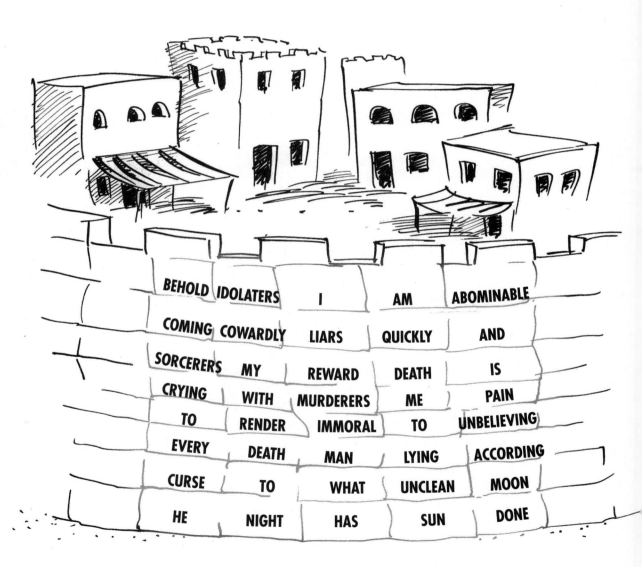

BEHOLD	IDOLATERS	I	AM	ABOMINABLE
COMING	COWARDLY	LIARS	QUICKLY	AND
SORCERERS	MY	REWARD	DEATH	IS
CRYING	WITH	MURDERERS	ME	PAIN
TO	RENDER	IMMORAL	TO	UNBELIEVING
EVERY	DEATH	MAN	LYING	ACCORDING
CURSE	TO	WHAT	UNCLEAN	MOON
HE	NIGHT	HAS	SUN	DONE

Once you've solved your puzzle, go to Revelation 22 to discover the reference for this week's verse.

" _____, _____ _____ _____,

____ _____ _____ _____ _____, _____

_____ _____ ___ _____ _____ _____

_____ _____ _____ _____ _____."

Revelation 22: _____

Way to go! Isn't this an awesome message?

GOD DWELLS WITH US

"Hey, Molly, did you know that there wouldn't be a sun or a moon in heaven?" Max looked over at Molly as she rubbed Sam's stomach.

"No, I didn't really realize it. I mean, I knew that Jesus was going to be its lamp, but I guess I didn't realize that there wouldn't be any sun or moon there. I can't wait to find out more about the new heaven and earth. Now that Sam is asleep, we can get to work."

Are you ready to find out more about the new heaven and earth? Don't forget to pray and then turn to page 198. Read Revelation 21:9-27 and mark the following key words by looking at your key-word bookmark:

Lamb†   angel   bowls (plagues)   I saw

holy city (New Jerusalem, the city)

Don't forget to mark your pronouns! Mark anything that tells you WHEN by drawing a green clock 🕐 or green circle ⭕.

Now discover what the angel shows John by asking the 5 W's and an H.

Revelation 21:10 WHAT does the angel show John?

_____

Revelation 21:11-26 Describe this holy city.

It has the _____ of God, her brilliance like a very _____ _____ of _____- clear _____. It had a great and high _____, with _____ _____, and at the gates _____ _____; and the names written on them were the _____ _____ of the sons of _____. There are _____ gates on the _____, _____ gates on the _____, _____ gates on the _____, and _____ gates on the _____. The _____ of the city had _____ foundation _____, and on them were the names of the _____ _____ of the _____.

The city is laid out as a _____, and its length and width are _____ hundred miles. Its wall is ____-_____ yards. The material of the wall was _____; and the city was pure _____, like _____ _____. The foundation stones of the city wall were adorned with every kind of precious stone: _____, _____, _____, _____, _____, _____, _____, _____, _____, _____, _____, and _____. And the twelve gates were _____ _____. The street of the city was _____ _____, like _____ _____. The Lord God and the Lamb are its _____. There is no _____ or _____ to shine on it. The _____ of God has _____ it, and its _____ is the Lamb. It is daytime because there is no _____ there. Its gates will never be _____ .

Revelation 21:27 WHO gets to come into the city?

_____

Isn't that *awesome?* Can you even imagine what it will look like? Draw a picture of the new Jerusalem in the box below from the description you have read.

```
┌─────────────────────────────────────────┐
│                                           │
│                                           │
│                                           │
│                                           │
│                                           │
│                                           │
│                                           │
│                                           │
│                                           │
│                                           │
│                                           │
│                                           │
│                                           │
└─────────────────────────────────────────┘
```

Now turn to your time line on page 54. Add this last event, "the new heaven and earth," on your time line after the great white throne judgment.

Wow! Jesus has made everything new. The old has passed away. There is no more sin, pain, crying, or death. We get to spend eternity with God and the Lamb!

WHAT IS IN THIS NEW CITY?

Look at what we have discovered about the new Jerusalem. WHAT a wonderful city! Have you ever heard the names of some of those jewels that are the foundation stones of the city? Can you imagine all those colors and the brilliance of those magnificent stones? WHAT else will be in this holy city? Let's find out as we begin our observations on Revelation 22. Turn to page 200. Read Revelation 22:1-6 and mark the following key words from your key-word bookmark:

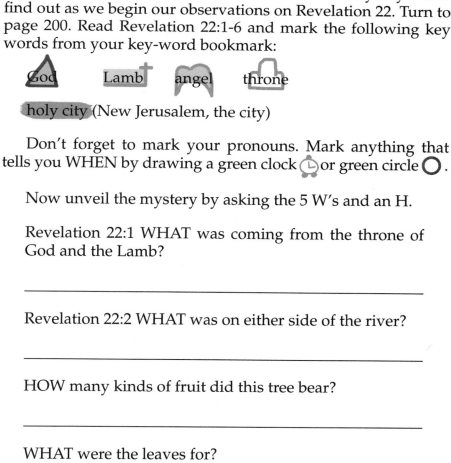

God   Lamb   angel   throne

holy city (New Jerusalem, the city)

Don't forget to mark your pronouns. Mark anything that tells you WHEN by drawing a green clock or green circle ○.

Now unveil the mystery by asking the 5 W's and an H.

Revelation 22:1 WHAT was coming from the throne of God and the Lamb?

_____

Revelation 22:2 WHAT was on either side of the river?

_____

HOW many kinds of fruit did this tree bear?

_____

WHAT were the leaves for?

_____

Revelation 22:3 WHAT is in the city?

_____

WHAT will His bond-servants do?

_____

Revelation 22:4 WHAT do you see about the bond-servants in this verse?

_____

Revelation 22:6 WHY did God send His angel?

_____

_____

Isn't this awesome? We will see Jesus' face, and His name will be on our foreheads! We can't wait! Now don't forget to practice your memory verse.

SERVING THE LAMB

Are you ready to enter into eternity to serve the Lamb? We are! There is just no way to imagine what it will really be like, but we know that God has given us some pretty fantastic things on this earth, and yet heaven will be much more than that—more than we can possibly think or imagine.

Today we are going to uncover what else the angel showed John in this awesome city and the last message to us in this precious book. So don't forget to pray. Then pull out your key-word bookmark and add the new key words listed below:

heed the words (box it in pink)

this book (color it brown)

churches (color it orange)

robes (color it yellow)

Turn to page 201. Read Revelation 22:7-21 and mark your new key words and the key words listed below on your Observation Worksheet:

 God   Jesus (or any description that refers to Jesus)

I am coming   holy city (New Jerusalem, the city)

 angel   worship   according to what he has done

Don't forget to mark your pronouns! Mark anything that tells you WHEN by drawing a green clock ⏰ or green circle ◯.

Now find out Jesus' last message. Ask the 5 W's and an H.

Revelation 22:7 WHO is blessed?

_____

Remember, "to heed" means to do! Do you remember our memory verse Revelation 1:3 from *Bible Prophecy for Kids*? If you don't, look it up now. Isn't it awesome!

Revelation 22:9 WHOM are we to worship?

_____

Revelation 22:10 WHAT did the angel tell John?

_____

WHY?

Because the _____ is _____.

Revelation 22:12 WHAT is with Jesus when He comes?

_____

WHAT is the reward given for?

_____

We have seen that those who go into the lake of fire are punished according to their deeds. Now we see that those who receive a reward receive it for the things they have done.

Are deeds—the things we do—important? Yes! We are not saved by our deeds. Salvation is a gift from God—we can't earn it (Ephesians 2:8-9). But the deeds we do show what has taken place in our hearts, that Jesus is in our lives. Believing in Jesus changes us, and our actions show that change. The way we live shows what we truly believe and if there has been a change in us.

When we are saved, we give our lives totally to God and live the way He wants us to live by loving Him and other people, sharing the gospel, meeting people's needs, studying His Word, and growing in our faith. All through Revelation we have seen how important our deeds are.

WHAT do your deeds say about you? Do they show that you have accepted God's Son in your life, or do you look just like the people in the world? WHAT kind of reward will you receive when Jesus returns?

_____

Revelation 22:14 WHAT do you need to do to be blessed?

_____

Do you know how to wash your robes? You're doing it right now by studying God's Word!

Revelation 22:14 WHAT do they receive?

_____

Revelation 22:17 WHAT do the Spirit and the bride say?

_____

Revelation 22:18 WHAT happens to anyone who adds to this book?

_____

Revelation 22:19 WHAT happens to anyone who takes away from this book?

_____

_____

Do you see how important the Book of Revelation is? We have been told we are blessed if we read, hear, and heed the words in it. John was told not to seal it up. God wants us to know what this book says, and we have just seen the consequences for adding to it or taking away from it.

You have just studied the book. Now WHAT will you do with it? Will you heed what you have studied and do it? Will it change the way you live? Will you be careful with these precious words of God and not try to make them fit what you want to believe, instead of what they say? His words are faithful and true. Heed the words that are written in this book.

Revelation 22:20 WHO is coming?

_____

Are you ready? Come, Lord Jesus! Come!

WHERE WILL YOU SPEND ETERNITY?

"Unbelievable!" Max exclaimed, as he looked up in the room of the new heaven and earth. "This is just unbelievable!"

Miss Kim smiled. "Molly, push that button right there on your left." Immediately the ceiling rolled back to reveal a skylight with a beautiful blue sky. A model of the holy city slowly started descending inside the room.

Molly stood with her mouth open. "Look at how brilliant the city is! Look at those 12 magnificent stones."

"Come over here," Miss Kim called. "You get to walk on the streets of gold, drink from the river, and pick fruit from these trees."

"Is the fruit real?"

"No, Molly, it isn't. Since this isn't really heaven, we don't have a tree that will bear 12 different fruits."

Molly giggled. "I was wondering. It looks awfully real. Look at how bright it is in here! It is so sparkling that it makes you never want to leave."

"That's what we wanted to accomplish," Miss Kim said with a smile. "A room that will make you think you have arrived in heaven. Well, guys, this is it. I want you to take some time and think about all you have experienced and let me know your ideas. You have done a fantastic job! There is one more thing for you to do before you are finished. You get to go into the last room. It is full of the things that take place during the end times like a seven-sealed scroll, small models of horses, trumpets, bowls, and all kinds of stuff. Use those objects and re-create the events of Revelation."

"All right," Max smiled. "This is going to be so much fun."

"But before you get started, remind yourself of the events by finding your way through the maze we have created of Revelation."

"Hey, Max, let's race to see who can finish their maze first."

"You're on, Molly! Let's go!"

Okay, Bible detectives, this is your last mystery to solve. Find your way through the maze by going through all the events that you have discovered "after these things" in Revelation.

There is only one way through the maze until you get to the end. And then, just like God gives us a choice, you have a choice about which path you will follow. There will be two ways to come out of the maze. One path leads to Jesus' 1,000-year reign, the new heaven and new earth, and eternity. The other leads to

death, the great white throne judgment, and the lake of fire and brimstone. When you come to the fork, choose which path you will take.

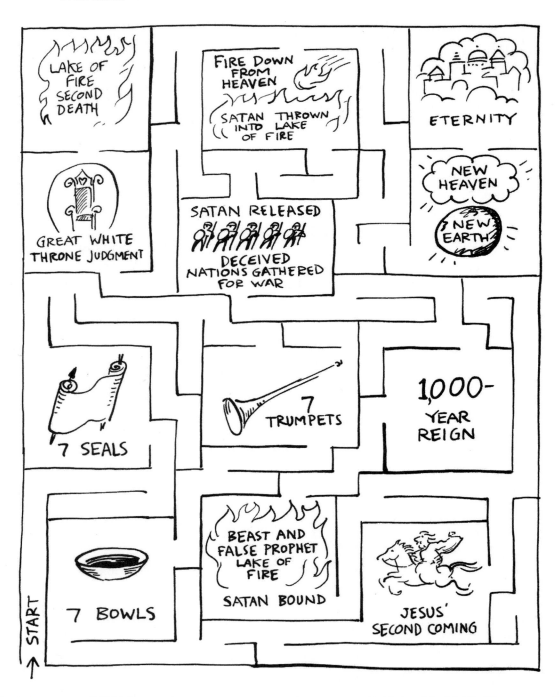

Way to go! Now let's do one last review. Look at the time line. It has all seven seals, trumpets, and bowls laid out for you. Put the names of the characters of Revelation where they belong on this time line.

WHERE do we see the two witnesses the first time in Revelation 11? Remember, these two witnesses prophesy and have the power of God for 3½ years before God allows them to be killed. Even though the Book of Revelation doesn't tell us when those 3½ years begin, we do know when they end (Revelation 11:7-14). Show WHERE our two witness go. Mark WHEN they are killed. HOW about the beast? WHERE do we see him for the first time?

WHEN is there a war in heaven and Satan (the dragon) is cast down to earth? WHERE does the woman of Revelation 12 go? WHERE does the dragon persecute the woman? WHERE do we see the beast (Revelation 13:5) given his authority, and for HOW long? WHERE does the second beast (the false prophet) go (Revelation 13:11-17)?

WHERE do we see the unholy three (the dragon, beast, and false prophet) when the three spirits come out of their mouths (Revelation 16:12-14)?

WHEN does Jesus return? And WHEN is Satan bound? WHEN are the beast and false prophet cast into the lake of fire (Revelation 19:20)? WHAT happens to Satan in the end, and WHERE does it go on the time line?

Place WHERE these people come on the scene and at WHAT event they leave the scene. Don't forget to also put WHEN the beast, the false prophet, and Satan end up in the lake of fire.

TiME LiNE

		Seven Seals								Seven Trumpets		
"After these things"	Lamb breaks seals	1	2	3	4	5	6	7	1	2	3	4

Seven Trumpets 3½ years			3½ years	Seven Bowls				
5	6		7	1	2	3	4	5

Seven Bowls					
6	7	Christ's 1,000-year reign	Great white throne judgment	New heaven New earth

WHAT an awesome job! We are so very proud of you! Now say that memory verse one more time to remind yourself that He is coming and His reward is with Him!

THE MYSTERY iS SOLVED!

Wow! You did it! You solved the mystery! You finished Revelation—a very important book of prophecy. Wasn't the Discovery Bible Museum the most fantastic museum you have ever seen? Just look at all you have discovered. You know that from the beginning of time until eternity an awesome God had a perfect plan!

You have seen just how much God loves you—so much that He would sacrifice His only Son to rescue you from the kingdom of darkness and from an eternity spent in the lake of fire and brimstone. Jesus is the slain Lamb in Revelation. Can you even imagine a love that powerful and strong?

As we uncovered the mysteries in Revelation, we saw that Revelation was God's message to the church to show the church the things that must soon take place. We saw that Jesus is the only One worthy to break the seven seals on the book. Then we heard the gallop of the horses as Jesus breaks the first seal and God's judgments begin on those who dwell on the earth. We saw that no matter how scary those earthquakes and plagues seem, the end will bring our conquering King on a white horse to restore our right to rule and reign with Him for all eternity!

Whose kingdom do you want to be in—God's or Satan's? Do you want to live for yourself, or live a life of dying to self to love and serve God? It's your choice. God has given us His Word so we can see just how much He loves us. He has a plan not only for our present lives, but also for all of eternity. *Amazing!*

As we wrap up this adventure, we pray that you will stand firm in the days ahead. Do not be afraid of what is to come in the future. It may seem scary, but just remember that God is in control. He has shown you what will happen in His Word. He is faithful! Keep your eyes on Jesus, and remember that He is coming very soon! Be ready. And don't ever forget this: WE WIN!

Don't forget to go to www.precept.org/D4Ycertificate to print your special certificate for completing this book. We are so very proud of you! Keep up the good work. We hope you'll join us for another adventure in God's Word real soon!

Molly, Max, and

(Sam)

P.S. Why don't you take this book to church or kids' camp? You can make your own Discovery Bible Museum using the ideas from the book and invite your parents and friends to discover the Revelation wing for themselves!

PUZZLE ANSWERS

Page 11

The rest of *mankind,* who were not *killed* by these *plagues,* did not *repent* of the works of their *hands,* so as not to *worship demons,* and the *idols* of *gold* and of *silver* and of *brass* and of *stone* and of *wood,* which can neither *see* nor *hear* nor *walk.*

Revelation 9:20

Page 30

⑪

⑥ ① S T R O N G

F H   ⑯

i U ⑬ H

④ R A i N B O W ⑦ B O O k

E N R O

⑫ ⑮ E ⑰ B i T T E R

⑭ M Y S T E R Y ⑤ T Y

E A ⑧ S E A ③

A T U C

⑩ P E A L S ② A N G E L

    O

    U

⑨ L A N D

145

Page 36

Then the seventh angel sounded; and there were loud voices in heaven, saying, "The kingdom of the world has become the kingdom of our Lord and of His Christ; and He will reign forever and ever."

Revelation 11:*15*

Page 44

Page 54

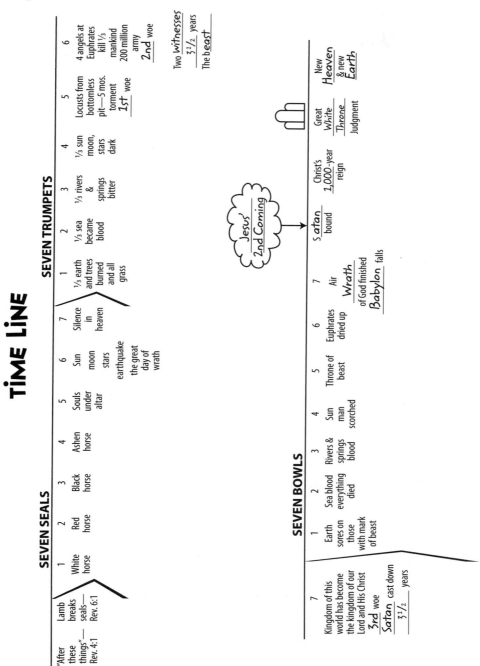

Page 59

"And the *smoke* of their *torment* goes up *forever* and *ever;* they have no *rest day* and *night,* those who *worship* the *beast* and his *image,* and whoever *receives* the *mark* of his *name.*"

Revelation 14:11

Page 78

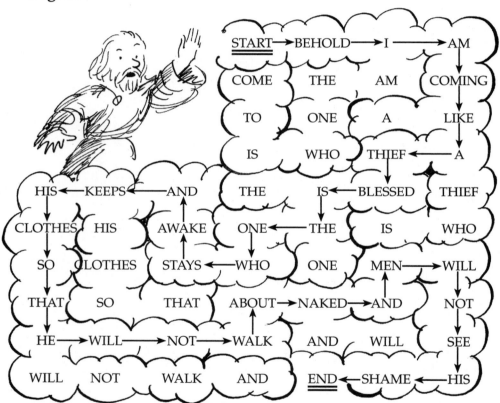

"Behold, I am coming like a thief. Blessed is the one who stays awake and keeps his clothes, so that he will not walk about naked and men will not see his shame."

Revelation 16:15

Page 79

Page 94

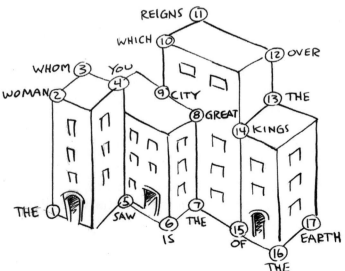

"The woman whom you saw is the great city, which reigns over the kings of the earth."

Revelation 17:18

Page 108

"From His mouth comes a sharp sword, so that with it He may strike down the nations, and He will rule them with a rod of iron; and He treads the wine press of the fierce wrath of God, the Almighty. And on His robe and on His thigh He has a name written, 'KING OF KINGS, AND LORD OF LORDS.'"

Revelation 19:15-16

Pages 129

"Behold, I am coming quickly, and My reward is with Me, to render to every man according to what he has done."

Revelation 22:12

page 140

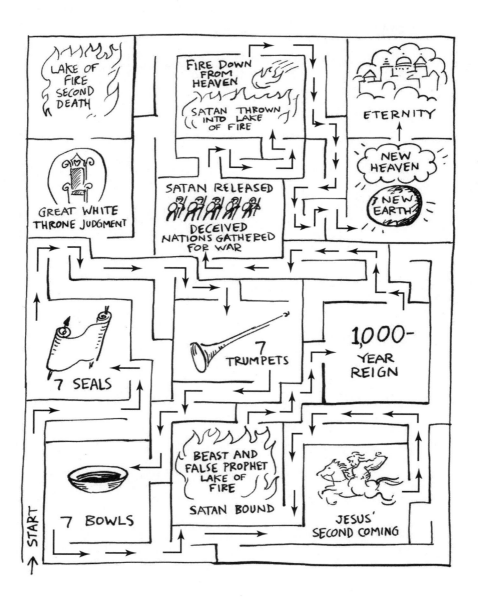

Page 142

TiME LiNE

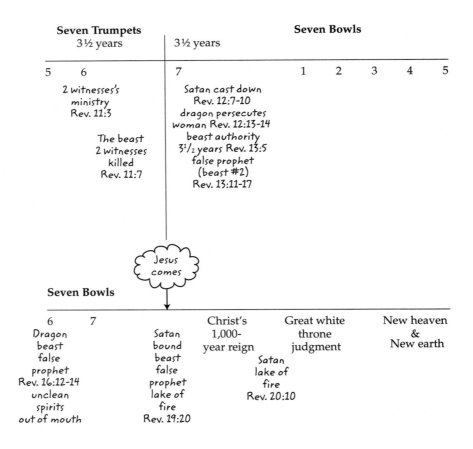

		Seven Seals								Seven Trumpets			
"After these things"	Lamb breaks seals	1	2	3	4	5	6	7	1	2	3	4

Seven Trumpets		Seven Bowls					
3½ years		3½ years					
5	6	7		1	2	3	4	5

6 — 2 witnesses's ministry Rev. 11:3

The beast 2 witnesses killed Rev. 11:7

7 — Satan cast down Rev. 12:7-10 dragon persecutes woman Rev. 12:13-14 beast authority $3\frac{1}{2}$ years Rev. 13:5 false prophet (beast #2) Rev. 13:11-17

Jesus comes

Seven Bowls

6	7		Christ's 1,000-year reign	Great white throne judgment	New heaven & New earth

6 — Dragon beast false prophet Rev. 16:12-14 unclean spirits out of mouth

Satan bound beast false prophet lake of fire Rev. 19:20

Satan lake of fire Rev. 20:10

KEY WORD LIST FOR REVELATION 8–22

God (draw a purple triangle and color it yellow)

Jesus (or any description that refers to Jesus like *the Lamb* and any pronouns) (draw a purple cross and color it yellow)

I saw (I looked) (color it blue)

throne (draw a throne and color it blue)

angel (draw blue wings or a blue angel and color it yellow)

seal (color it orange)

prayers (draw a purple and color it pink)

trumpet (sound, sounded, blasts when it refers to the trumpets) (color it yellow)

those who dwell on the earth (color it green)

woe (circle it in black and color it brown)

seal, sealed (this is the seal that refers to the people whom God sealed, not the seven seals) (draw a purple S)

worship (circle it in purple and color it blue)

repent (draw a red arrow and color it yellow)

book (draw a brown scroll)

thunder (draw a black lightning bolt)

mystery (box it in orange and color it green)

two witnesses (and any synonyms that refer to them, such as *two olive trees* or *two lampstands*) (color it blue)

beast (color it brown)

make war (wage war, any reference to war) (circle it in black)

wrath (draw a red *w*)

kingdom (kings) (draw a purple crown and color it blue)

sign (draw a red sign)

woman (color it blue)

woman's child (box it in purple)

wilderness (color it orange)

dragon (devil, serpent, Satan) (draw a red pitchfork)

was thrown down (has been thrown down, etc.) (color it green)

overcome (overcame) (color it yellow)

another beast (color it orange)

the image of the beast (mark of the beast) (draw a red 666 over it)

Babylon (great harlot, woman, great city, mother of harlots) (color it red)

gospel (draw a red megaphone and color it green)

Spirit (draw a purple ⌣⌣⌣ and color it yellow)

temple (color it purple)

plagues (bowls) (color it pink)

I am coming (draw a purple cloud around it and color it in three parts: the first part blue, the middle part yellow, and the last part blue)

demons (draw red pitchfork)

false prophet (color it orange)

deeds (draw green feet)

bride (box it in purple)

lake of fire (draw and color it like fire)

the dead (color it black)

first resurrection (circle it in green and color it pink)

second death (underline it twice in black)

according to their deeds (according to what he has done) (circle it in green and color it green)

holy city (New Jerusalem, the city) (color it purple)

heed the words (box it in pink)

this book (color it brown)

churches (color it orange)

robes (color it yellow)

Remember: Mark WHERE by double-underlining the WHERE in green. And mark anything that tells you WHEN by drawing a green clock 🕐 or green circle like this: ⭕

OBSERVATION WORKSHEETS
REVELATION 6–22

Chapter 6

1 Then I saw when the Lamb broke one of the seven seals, and I heard one of the four living creatures saying as with a voice of thunder, "Come."

2 I looked, and behold, a white horse, and he who sat on it had a bow; and a crown was given to him, and he went out conquering and to conquer.

3 When He broke the second seal, I heard the second living creature saying, "Come."

4 And another, a red horse, went out; and to him who sat on it, it was granted to take peace from the earth, and that *men* would slay one another; and a great sword was given to him.

5 When He broke the third seal, I heard the third living creature saying, "Come." I looked, and behold, a black horse; and he who sat on it had a pair of scales in his hand.

6 And I heard *something* like a voice in the center of the four living creatures saying, "A quart of wheat for a denarius, and three quarts of barley for a denarius; and do not damage the oil and the wine."

7 When the Lamb broke the fourth seal, I heard the voice of the fourth living creature saying, "Come."

8 I looked, and behold, an ashen horse; and he who sat on it had the name Death; and Hades was following with him. Authority was given to them over a fourth of the earth, to kill with sword and with famine and with pestilence and by the wild beasts of the earth.

9 When the Lamb broke the fifth seal, I saw underneath the altar the souls of those who had been slain because of the word of God, and because of the testimony which they had maintained; 10 and they cried out with a loud voice, saying, "How long, O Lord, holy and true, will You refrain from judging and avenging our blood on those who dwell on the earth?"

11 And there was given to each of them a white robe; and they were told that they should rest for a little while longer, until *the number of* their fellow servants and their brethren who were to be killed even as they had been, would be completed also.

12 I looked when He broke the sixth seal, and there was a great earthquake; and the sun became black as sackcloth *made* of hair, and the whole moon became like blood;

13 and the stars of the sky fell to the earth, as a fig tree casts its unripe figs when shaken by a great wind.

14 The sky was split apart like a scroll when it is rolled up, and every mountain and island were moved out of their places.

15 Then the kings of the earth and the great men and the commanders and the rich and the strong and every slave and free man hid themselves in the caves and among the rocks of the mountains;

16 and they said to the mountains and to the rocks, "Fall on us and hide us from the presence of Him who sits on the throne, and from the wrath of the Lamb;

17 for the great day of their wrath has come, and who is able to stand?"

Chapter 7

1 After this I saw four angels standing at the four corners of the earth, holding back the four winds of the earth, so that no wind would blow on the earth or on the sea or on any tree.

2 And I saw another angel ascending from the rising of the sun, having the seal of the living God; and he cried out with a loud voice to the four angels to whom it was granted to harm the earth and the sea,

3 saying, "Do not harm the earth or the sea or the trees until we have sealed the bond-servants of our God on their fore-heads."

4 And I heard the number of those who were sealed, one hundred and forty-four thousand sealed from every tribe of the sons of Israel:

5 from the tribe of Judah, twelve thousand *were* sealed, from the tribe of Reuben twelve thousand, from the tribe of Gad twelve thousand,

6 from the tribe of Asher twelve thousand, from the tribe of Naphtali twelve thousand, from the tribe of Manasseh twelve thousand,

7 from the tribe of Simeon twelve thousand, from the tribe of Levi twelve thousand, from the tribe of Issachar twelve thou-sand,

8 from the tribe of Zebulun twelve thousand, from the tribe

of Joseph twelve thousand, from the tribe of Benjamin, twelve thousand *were* sealed.

9 After these things I looked, and behold, a great multitude which no one could count, from every nation and *all* tribes and peoples and tongues, standing before the throne and before the Lamb, clothed in white robes, and palm branches *were* in their hands;

10 and they cry out with a loud voice, saying, "Salvation to our God who sits on the throne, and to the Lamb."

11 And all the angels were standing around the throne and *around* the elders and the four living creatures; and they fell on their faces before the throne and worshiped God,

12 saying,

"Amen, blessing and glory and wisdom and thanksgiving and honor and power and might, *be* to our God forever and ever. Amen."

13 Then one of the elders answered, saying to me, "These who are clothed in the white robes, who are they, and where have they come from?"

14 I said to him, "My lord, you know." And he said to me, "These are the ones who come out of the great tribulation,

and they have washed their robes and made them white in
the blood of the Lamb.

15 "For this reason, they are before the throne of God; and
they serve Him day and night in His temple; and He who sits
on the throne will spread His tabernacle over them.

16 "They will hunger no longer, nor thirst anymore; nor will
the sun beat down on them, nor any heat;

17 for the Lamb in the center of the throne will be their shepherd, and will guide them to springs of the water of life; and
God will wipe every tear from their eyes."

Chapter 8

1 When the Lamb broke the seventh seal, there was silence in
heaven for about half an hour.

2 And I saw the seven angels who stand before God, and
seven trumpets were given to them.

3 Another angel came and stood at the altar, holding a
golden censer; and much incense was given to him, so that he
might add it to the prayers of all the saints on the golden altar
which was before the throne.

4 And the smoke of the incense, with the prayers of the
saints, went up before God out of the angel's hand.

5 Then the angel took the censer and filled it with the fire of the altar, and threw it to the earth; and there followed peals of thunder and sounds and flashes of lightning and an earthquake.

6 And the seven angels who had the seven trumpets prepared themselves to sound them.

7 The first sounded, and there came hail and fire, mixed with blood, and they were thrown to the earth; and a third of the earth was burned up, and a third of the trees were burned up, and all the green grass was burned up.

8 The second angel sounded, and *something* like a great mountain burning with fire was thrown into the sea; and a third of the sea became blood,

9 and a third of the creatures which were in the sea and had life, died; and a third of the ships were destroyed.

10 The third angel sounded, and a great star fell from heaven, burning like a torch, and it fell on a third of the rivers and on the springs of waters.

11The name of the star is called Wormwood; and a third of the waters became wormwood, and many men died from the waters, because they were made bitter.

12 The fourth angel sounded, and a third of the sun and a third of the moon and a third of the stars were struck, so that a third of them would be darkened and the day would not shine for a third of it, and the night in the same way.

13 Then I looked, and I heard an eagle flying in midheaven, saying with a loud voice, "Woe, woe, woe to those who dwell on the earth, because of the remaining blasts of the trumpet of the three angels who are about to sound!"

Chapter 9

1 Then the fifth angel sounded, and I saw a star from heaven which had fallen to the earth; and the key of the bottomless pit was given to him.

2 He opened the bottomless pit, and smoke went up out of the pit, like the smoke of a great furnace; and the sun and the air were darkened by the smoke of the pit.

3 Then out of the smoke came locusts upon the earth, and power was given them, as the scorpions of the earth have power.

4 They were told not to hurt the grass of the earth, nor any green thing, nor any tree, but only the men who do not have the seal of God on their foreheads.

5 And they were not permitted to kill anyone, but to torment for five months; and their torment was like the torment of a scorpion when it stings a man.

6 And in those days men will seek death and will not find it; they will long to die, and death flees from them.

7 The appearance of the locusts was like horses prepared for battle; and on their heads appeared to be crowns like gold, and their faces were like the faces of men.

8 They had hair like the hair of women, and their teeth were like *the teeth* of lions.

9 They had breastplates like breastplates of iron; and the sound of their wings was like the sound of chariots, of many horses rushing to battle.

10 They have tails like scorpions, and stings; and in their tails is their power to hurt men for five months.

11 They have as king over them, the angel of the abyss; his name in Hebrew is Abaddon, and in the Greek he has the name Apollyon.

12 The first woe is past; behold, two woes are still coming after these things.

13 Then the sixth angel sounded, and I heard a voice from the four horns of the golden altar which is before God,

14 one saying to the sixth angel who had the trumpet, "Release the four angels who are bound at the great river Euphrates."

15 And the four angels, who had been prepared for the hour and day and month and year, were released, so that they would kill a third of mankind.

16 The number of the armies of the horsemen was two hundred million; I heard the number of them.

17 And this is how I saw in the vision the horses and those who sat on them: *the riders* had breastplates *the color* of fire and of hyacinth and of brimstone; and the heads of the horses are like the heads of lions; and out of their mouths proceed fire and smoke and brimstone.

18 A third of mankind was killed by these three plagues, by the fire and the smoke and the brimstone which proceeded out of their mouths.

19 For the power of the horses is in their mouths and in their tails; for their tails are like serpents and have heads, and with them they do harm.

20 The rest of mankind, who were not killed by these plagues, did not repent of the works of their hands, so as not to worship demons, and the idols of gold and of silver and of brass and of stone and of wood, which can neither see nor hear nor walk;

21 and they did not repent of their murders nor of their sorceries nor of their immorality nor of their thefts.

Chapter 10

1 I saw another strong angel coming down out of heaven, clothed with a cloud; and the rainbow was upon his head, and his face was like the sun, and his feet like pillars of fire;

2 and he had in his hand a little book which was open. He placed his right foot on the sea and his left on the land;

3 and he cried out with a loud voice, as when a lion roars; and when he had cried out, the seven peals of thunder uttered their voices.

4 When the seven peals of thunder had spoken, I was about to write; and I heard a voice from heaven saying, "Seal up the things which the seven peals of thunder have spoken and do not write them."

5 Then the angel whom I saw standing on the sea and on the land lifted up his right hand to heaven,

6 and swore by Him who lives forever and ever, WHO CREATED HEAVEN AND THE THINGS IN IT, AND THE EARTH AND THE THINGS IN IT, AND THE SEA AND THE THINGS IN IT, that there will be delay no longer,

7 but in the days of the voice of the seventh angel, when he is about to sound, then the mystery of God is finished, as He preached to His servants the prophets.

8 Then the voice which I heard from heaven, *I heard* again speaking with me, and saying, "Go, take the book which is open in the hand of the angel who stands on the sea and on the land."

9 So I went to the angel, telling him to give me the little book. And he said to me, "Take it and eat it; it will make your stomach bitter, but in your mouth it will be sweet as honey."

10 I took the little book out of the angel's hand and ate it, and in my mouth it was sweet as honey; and when I had eaten it, my stomach was made bitter.

11And they said to me, "You must prophesy again concerning many peoples and nations and tongues and kings."

Chapter 11

1 Then there was given me a measuring rod like a staff; and someone said, "Get up and measure the temple of God and the altar, and those who worship in it.

2 "Leave out the court which is outside the temple and do not measure it, for it has been given to the nations; and they will tread under foot the holy city for forty-two months.

3 "And I will grant *authority* to my two witnesses, and they will prophesy for twelve hundred and sixty days, clothed in sackcloth."

4 These are the two olive trees and the two lampstands that stand before the Lord of the earth.

5 And if anyone wants to harm them, fire flows out of their mouth and devours their enemies; so if anyone wants to harm them, he must be killed in this way.

6 These have the power to shut up the sky, so that rain will not fall during the days of their prophesying; and they have power over the waters to turn them into blood, and to strike the earth with every plague, as often as they desire.

7 When they have finished their testimony, the beast that

comes up out of the abyss will make war with them, and overcome them and kill them.

8 And their dead bodies *will lie* in the street of the great city which mystically is called Sodom and Egypt, where also their Lord was crucified.

9 Those from the peoples and tribes and tongues and nations *will* look at their dead bodies for three and a half days, and will not permit their dead bodies to be laid in a tomb.

10 And those who dwell on the earth *will* rejoice over them and celebrate; and they will send gifts to one another, because these two prophets tormented those who dwell on the earth.

11 But after the three and a half days, the breath of life from God came into them, and they stood on their feet; and great fear fell upon those who were watching them.

12 And they heard a loud voice from heaven saying to them, "Come up here." Then they went up into heaven in the cloud, and their enemies watched them.

13 And in that hour there was a great earthquake, and a tenth of the city fell; seven thousand people were killed in the earth-quake, and the rest were terrified and gave glory to the God of heaven.

14 The second woe is past; behold, the third woe is coming quickly.

15 Then the seventh angel sounded; and there were loud voices in heaven, saying,

"The kingdom of the world has become *the kingdom* of our Lord and of His Christ; and He will reign forever and ever."

16 And the twenty-four elders, who sit on their thrones before God, fell on their faces and worshiped God,

17 saying,

"We give You thanks, O Lord God, the Almighty, who are and who were, because You have taken Your great power and have begun to reign.

18 "And the nations were enraged, and Your wrath came, and the time *came* for the dead to be judged, and *the time* to reward Your bond-servants the prophets and the saints and those who fear Your name, the small and the great, and to destroy those who destroy the earth."

19 And the temple of God which is in heaven was opened; and the ark of His covenant appeared in His temple, and there were flashes of lightning and sounds and peals of thunder and an earthquake and a great hailstorm.

Chapter 12

1 A great sign appeared in heaven: a woman clothed with the sun, and the moon under her feet, and on her head a crown of twelve stars;

2 and she was with child; and she cried out, being in labor and in pain to give birth.

3 Then another sign appeared in heaven: and behold, a great red dragon having seven heads and ten horns, and on his heads *were* seven diadems.

4 And his tail swept away a third of the stars of heaven and threw them to the earth. And the dragon stood before the woman who was about to give birth, so that when she gave birth he might devour her child.

5 And she gave birth to a son, a male *child*, who is to rule all the nations with a rod of iron; and her child was caught up to God and to His throne.

6 Then the woman fled into the wilderness where she had a place prepared by God, so that there she would be nourished for one thousand two hundred and sixty days.

7 And there was war in heaven, Michael and his angels

waging war with the dragon. The dragon and his angels waged war,

8 and they were not strong enough, and there was no longer a place found for them in heaven.

9 And the great dragon was thrown down, the serpent of old who is called the devil and Satan, who deceives the whole world; he was thrown down to the earth, and his angels were thrown down with him.

10 Then I heard a loud voice in heaven, saying, "Now the salvation, and the power, and the kingdom of our God and the authority of His Christ have come, for the accuser of our brethren has been thrown down, he who accuses them before our God day and night.

11 "And they overcame him because of the blood of the Lamb and because of the word of their testimony, and they did not love their life even when faced with death.

12 "For this reason, rejoice, O heavens and you who dwell in them. Woe to the earth and the sea, because the devil has come down to you, having great wrath, knowing that he has *only* a short time."

13 And when the dragon saw that he was thrown down to the

earth, he persecuted the woman who gave birth to the male

child.

14 But the two wings of the great eagle were given to the

woman, so that she could fly into the wilderness to her place,

where she was nourished for a time and times and half a time,

from the presence of the serpent.

15 And the serpent poured water like a river out of his mouth

after the woman, so that he might cause her to be swept away

with the flood.

16 But the earth helped the woman, and the earth opened its

mouth and drank up the river which the dragon poured out

of his mouth.

17 So the dragon was enraged with the woman, and went

off to make war with the rest of her children, who keep the

commandments of God and hold to the testimony of Jesus.

Chapter 13

1 And the dragon stood on the sand of the seashore.

Then I saw a beast coming up out of the sea, having ten horns

and seven heads, and on his horns were ten diadems, and on

his heads were blasphemous names.

2 And the beast which I saw was like a leopard, and his feet

were like *those* of a bear, and his mouth like the mouth of a lion. And the dragon gave him his power and his throne and great authority.

3 *I saw* one of his heads as if it had been slain, and his fatal wound was healed. And the whole earth was amazed *and followed* after the beast;

4 they worshiped the dragon because he gave his authority to the beast; and they worshiped the beast, saying, "Who is like the beast, and who is able to wage war with him?"

5 There was given to him a mouth speaking arrogant words and blasphemies, and authority to act for forty-two months was given to him.

6 And he opened his mouth in blasphemies against God, to blaspheme His name and His tabernacle, *that is,* those who dwell in heaven.

7 It was also given to him to make war with the saints and to overcome them, and authority over every tribe and people and tongue and nation was given to him.

8 All who dwell on the earth will worship him, *everyone* whose name has not been written from the foundation of the world in the book of life of the Lamb who has been slain.

9 If anyone has an ear, let him hear.

10 If anyone *is destined* for captivity, to captivity he goes;

if anyone kills with the sword, with the sword he must be

killed. Here is the perseverance and the faith of the saints.

11 Then I saw another beast coming up out of the earth; and

he had two horns like a lamb and he spoke as a dragon.

12 He exercises all the authority of the first beast in his pres-

ence. And he makes the earth and those who dwell in it to

worship the first beast, whose fatal wound was healed.

13 He performs great signs, so that he even makes fire come

down out of heaven to the earth in the presence of men.

14 And he deceives those who dwell on the earth because of

the signs which it was given him to perform in the presence

of the beast, telling those who dwell on the earth to make an

image to the beast who had the wound of the sword and has

come to life.

15 And it was given to him to give breath to the image of the

beast, so that the image of the beast would even speak and

cause as many as do not worship the image of the beast to be

killed.

16 And he causes all, the small and the great, and the rich and

the poor, and the free men and the slaves, to be given a mark on their right hand or on their forehead,

17 and *he provides* that no one will be able to buy or to sell, except the one who has the mark, *either* the name of the beast or the number of his name.

18 Here is wisdom. Let him who has understanding calculate the number of the beast, for the number is that of a man; and his number is six hundred and sixty-six.

Chapter 14

1 Then I looked, and behold, the Lamb *was* standing on Mount Zion, and with Him one hundred and forty-four thousand, having His name and the name of His Father written on their foreheads.

2 And I heard a voice from heaven, like the sound of many waters and like the sound of loud thunder, and the voice which I heard *was* like *the sound* of harpists playing on their harps.

3 And they sang a new song before the throne and before the four living creatures and the elders; and no one could learn the song except the one hundred and forty-four thousand who had been purchased from the earth.

4 These are the ones who have not been defiled with women, for they have kept themselves chaste. These *are* the ones who follow the Lamb wherever He goes. These have been purchased from among men as first fruits to God and to the Lamb.

5 And no lie was found in their mouth; they are blameless.

6 And I saw another angel flying in midheaven, having an eternal gospel to preach to those who live on the earth, and to every nation and tribe and tongue and people;

7 and he said with a loud voice, "Fear God, and give Him glory, because the hour of His judgment has come; worship Him who made the heaven and the earth and sea and springs of waters."

8 And another angel, a second one, followed, saying, "Fallen, fallen is Babylon the great, she who has made all the nations drink of the wine of the passion of her immorality."

9 Then another angel, a third one, followed them, saying with a loud voice, "If anyone worships the beast and his image, and receives a mark on his forehead or on his hand, 10 he also will drink of the wine of the wrath of God, which is mixed in full strength in the cup of His anger; and he will be

tormented with fire and brimstone in the presence of the holy angels and in the presence of the Lamb.

11"And the smoke of their torment goes up forever and ever; they have no rest day and night, those who worship the beast and his image, and whoever receives the mark of his name."

12 Here is the perseverance of the saints who keep the commandments of God and their faith in Jesus.

13 And I heard a voice from heaven, saying, "Write, 'Blessed are the dead who die in the Lord from now on!'" "Yes," says the Spirit, "so that they may rest from their labors, for their deeds follow with them."

14 Then I looked, and behold, a white cloud, and sitting on the cloud *was* one like a son of man, having a golden crown on His head and a sharp sickle in His hand.

15 And another angel came out of the temple, crying out with a loud voice to Him who sat on the cloud, "Put in your sickle and reap, for the hour to reap has come, because the harvest of the earth is ripe."

16 Then He who sat on the cloud swung His sickle over the earth, and the earth was reaped.

17 And another angel came out of the temple which is in heaven, and he also had a sharp sickle.

18 Then another angel, the one who has power over fire, came out from the altar; and he called with a loud voice to him who had the sharp sickle, saying, "Put in your sharp sickle and gather the clusters from the vine of the earth, because her grapes are ripe."

19 So the angel swung his sickle to the earth and gathered *the clusters from* the vine of the earth, and threw them into the great wine press of the wrath of God.

20 And the wine press was trodden outside the city, and blood came out from the wine press, up to the horses' bridles, for a distance of two hundred miles.

Chapter 15

1 Then I saw another sign in heaven, great and marvelous, seven angels who had seven plagues, which are the last, because in them the wrath of God is finished.

2 And I saw something like a sea of glass mixed with fire, and those who had been victorious over the beast and his image and the number of his name, standing on the sea of glass, holding harps of God.

3 And they sang the song of Moses, the bond-servant of God,

and the song of the Lamb, saying,

"Great and marvelous are Your works,

O Lord God, the Almighty;

Righteous and true are Your ways,

King of the nations!

4 "Who will not fear, O Lord, and glorify Your name?

For You alone are holy;

For ALL THE NATIONS WILL COME AND WORSHIP BEFORE YOU,

FOR YOUR RIGHTEOUS ACTS HAVE BEEN REVEALED."

5 After these things I looked, and the temple of the taber-

nacle of testimony in heaven was opened,

6 and the seven angels who had the seven plagues came out

of the temple, clothed in linen, clean *and* bright, and girded

around their chests with golden sashes.

7 Then one of the four living creatures gave to the seven

angels seven golden bowls full of the wrath of God, who lives

forever and ever.

8 And the temple was filled with smoke from the glory

of God and from His power; and no one was able to enter

the temple until the seven plagues of the seven angels were finished.

Chapter 16

1 Then I heard a loud voice from the temple, saying to the seven angels, "Go and pour out on the earth the seven bowls of the wrath of God."

2 So the first *angel* went and poured out his bowl on the earth; and it became a loathsome and malignant sore on the people who had the mark of the beast and who worshiped his image.

3 The second *angel* poured out his bowl into the sea, and it became blood like *that* of a dead man; and every living thing in the sea died.

4 Then the third *angel* poured out his bowl into the rivers and the springs of waters; and they became blood.

5 And I heard the angel of the waters saying, "Righteous are You, who are and who were, O Holy One, because You judged these things;

6 for they poured out the blood of saints and prophets, and You have given them blood to drink. They deserve it."

7 And I heard the altar saying, "Yes, O Lord God, the Almighty, true and righteous are Your judgments."

8 The fourth *angel* poured out his bowl upon the sun, and it was given to it to scorch men with fire.

9 Men were scorched with fierce heat; and they blasphemed the name of God who has the power over these plagues, and they did not repent so as to give Him glory.

10 Then the fifth *angel* poured out his bowl on the throne of the beast, and his kingdom became darkened; and they gnawed their tongues because of pain,

11and they blasphemed the God of heaven because of their pains and their sores; and they did not repent of their deeds.

12 The sixth *angel* poured out his bowl on the great river, the Euphrates; and its water was dried up, so that the way would be prepared for the kings from the east.

13 And I saw *coming* out of the mouth of the dragon and out of the mouth of the beast and out of the mouth of the false prophet, three unclean spirits like frogs;

14 for they are spirits of demons, performing signs, which go out to the kings of the whole world, to gather them together for the war of the great day of God, the Almighty.

15 ("Behold, I am coming like a thief. Blessed is the one who stays awake and keeps his clothes, so that he will not walk about naked and men will not see his shame.")

16 And they gathered them together to the place which in Hebrew is called Har-Magedon.

17 Then the seventh *angel* poured out his bowl upon the air, and a loud voice came out of the temple from the throne, saying, "It is done."

18 And there were flashes of lightning and sounds and peals of thunder; and there was a great earthquake, such as there had not been since man came to be upon the earth, so great an earthquake *was it, and* so mighty.

19 The great city was split into three parts, and the cities of the nations fell. Babylon the great was remembered before God, to give her the cup of the wine of His fierce wrath.

20 And every island fled away, and the mountains were not found.

21 And huge hailstones, about one hundred pounds each, came down from heaven upon men; and men blasphemed God because of the plague of the hail, because its plague was extremely severe.

Chapter 17

1 Then one of the seven angels who had the seven bowls
came and spoke with me, saying, "Come here, I will show
you the judgment of the great harlot who sits on many waters,

2 with whom the kings of the earth committed *acts of*
immorality, and those who dwell on the earth were made
drunk with the wine of her immorality."

3 And he carried me away in the Spirit into a wilderness;
and I saw a woman sitting on a scarlet beast, full of blasphemous names, having seven heads and ten horns.

4 The woman was clothed in purple and scarlet, and
adorned with gold and precious stones and pearls, having in
her hand a gold cup full of abominations and of the unclean
things of her immorality,

5 and on her forehead a name *was* written, a mystery,
"BABYLON THE GREAT, THE MOTHER OF HARLOTS
AND OF THE ABOMINATIONS OF THE EARTH."

6 And I saw the woman drunk with the blood of the saints,
and with the blood of the witnesses of Jesus. When I saw her,
I wondered greatly.

7 And the angel said to me, "Why do you wonder? I will tell

you the mystery of the woman and of the beast that carries her, which has the seven heads and the ten horns.

8 "The beast that you saw was, and is not, and is about to come up out of the abyss and go to destruction. And those who dwell on the earth, whose name has not been written in the book of life from the foundation of the world, will wonder when they see the beast, that he was and is not and will come.

9 "Here is the mind which has wisdom. The seven heads are seven mountains on which the woman sits,

10 and they are seven kings; five have fallen, one is, the other has not yet come; and when he comes, he must remain a little while.

11"The beast which was and is not, is himself also an eighth and is *one* of the seven, and he goes to destruction.

12 "The ten horns which you saw are ten kings who have not yet received a kingdom, but they receive authority as kings with the beast for one hour.

13 "These have one purpose, and they give their power and authority to the beast.

14 "These will wage war against the Lamb, and the Lamb will overcome them, because He is Lord of lords and King of

kings, and those who are with Him *are the* called and chosen and faithful."

15 And he said to me, "The waters which you saw where the harlot sits, are peoples and multitudes and nations and tongues.

16 "And the ten horns which you saw, and the beast, these will hate the harlot and will make her desolate and naked, and will eat her flesh and will burn her up with fire.

17 "For God has put it in their hearts to execute His purpose by having a common purpose, and by giving their kingdom to the beast, until the words of God will be fulfilled.

18 "The woman whom you saw is the great city, which reigns over the kings of the earth."

Chapter 18

1 After these things I saw another angel coming down from heaven, having great authority, and the earth was illumined with his glory.

2 And he cried out with a mighty voice, saying, "Fallen, fallen is Babylon the great! She has become a dwelling place of demons and a prison of every unclean spirit, and a prison of every unclean and hateful bird.

3 "For all the nations have drunk of the wine of the passion of her immorality, and the kings of the earth have committed *acts of* immorality with her, and the merchants of the earth have become rich by the wealth of her sensuality."

4 I heard another voice from heaven, saying, "Come out of her, my people, so that you will not participate in her sins and receive of her plagues;

5 for her sins have piled up as high as heaven, and God has remembered her iniquities.

6 "Pay her back even as she has paid, and give back *to her* double according to her deeds; in the cup which she has mixed, mix twice as much for her.

7 "To the degree that she glorified herself and lived sensuously, to the same degree give her torment and mourning; for she says in her heart, 'I SIT *as* A QUEEN AND I AM NOT A WIDOW, and will never see mourning.'

8 "For this reason in one day her plagues will come, pestilence and mourning and famine, and she will be burned up with fire; for the Lord God who judges her is strong.

9 "And the kings of the earth, who committed *acts of* immo-

rality and lived sensuously with her, will weep and lament over her when they see the smoke of her burning,

10 standing at a distance because of the fear of her torment, saying, 'Woe, woe, the great city, Babylon, the strong city! For in one hour your judgment has come.'

11 "And the merchants of the earth weep and mourn over her, because no one buys their cargoes any more—

12 cargoes of gold and silver and precious stones and pearls and fine linen and purple and silk and scarlet, and every *kind of* citron wood and every article of ivory and every article *made* from very costly wood and bronze and iron and marble,

13 and cinnamon and spice and incense and perfume and frankincense and wine and olive oil and fine flour and wheat and cattle and sheep, and *cargoes* of horses and chariots and slaves and human lives.

14 "The fruit you long for has gone from you, and all things that were luxurious and splendid have passed away from you and *men* will no longer find them.

15 "The merchants of these things, who became rich from her, will stand at a distance because of the fear of her torment, weeping and mourning,

16 saying, 'Woe, woe, the great city, she who was clothed in fine linen and purple and scarlet, and adorned with gold and precious stones and pearls;

17 for in one hour such great wealth has been laid waste!' And every shipmaster and every passenger and sailor, and as many as make their living by the sea, stood at a distance,

18 and were crying out as they saw the smoke of her burning, saying, 'What *city* is like the great city?'

19 "And they threw dust on their heads and were crying out, weeping and mourning, saying, 'Woe, woe, the great city, in which all who had ships at sea became rich by her wealth, for in one hour she has been laid waste!'

20 "Rejoice over her, O heaven, and you saints and apostles and prophets, because God has pronounced judgment for you against her."

21 Then a strong angel took up a stone like a great millstone and threw it into the sea, saying, "So will Babylon, the great city, be thrown down with violence, and will not be found any longer.

22 "And the sound of harpists and musicians and flute-play-ers and trumpeters will not be heard in you any longer; and

no craftsman of any craft will be found in you any longer; and

the sound of a mill will not be heard in you any longer;

23 and the light of a lamp will not shine in you any longer;

and the voice of the bridegroom and bride will not be heard

in you any longer; for your merchants were the great men

of the earth, because all the nations were deceived by your

sorcery.

24 "And in her was found the blood of prophets and of saints

and of all who have been slain on the earth."

Chapter 19

1 After these things I heard something like a loud voice of a

great multitude in heaven, saying,

"Hallelujah! Salvation and glory and power belong to our

God;

2 BECAUSE HIS JUDGMENTS ARE TRUE AND RIGHTEOUS; for He

has judged the great harlot who was corrupting the earth with

her immorality, and HE HAS AVENGED THE BLOOD OF HIS BOND-

SERVANTS ON HER."

3 And a second time they said, "Hallelujah! HER SMOKE RISES

UP FOREVER AND EVER."

4 And the twenty-four elders and the four living creatures

fell down and worshiped God who sits on the throne saying,

"Amen. Hallelujah!"

5 And a voice came from the throne, saying,

"Give praise to our God, all you His bond-servants, you who

fear Him, the small and the great."

6 Then I heard *something* like the voice of a great multitude

and like the sound of many waters and like the sound of

mighty peals of thunder, saying,

"Hallelujah! For the Lord our God, the Almighty, reigns.

7 "Let us rejoice and be glad and give the glory to Him, for

the marriage of the Lamb has come and His bride has made

herself ready."

8 It was given to her to clothe herself in fine linen, bright *and*

clean; for the fine linen is the righteous acts of the saints.

9 Then he said to me, "Write, 'Blessed are those who are

invited to the marriage supper of the Lamb.'" And he said to

me, "These are true words of God."

10 Then I fell at his feet to worship him. But he said to me,

"Do not do that; I am a fellow servant of yours and your

brethren who hold the testimony of Jesus; worship God. For

the testimony of Jesus is the spirit of prophecy."

11And I saw heaven opened, and behold, a white horse, and He who sat on it *is* called Faithful and True, and in righteousness He judges and wages war.

12 His eyes *are* a flame of fire, and on His head *are* many diadems; and He has a name written *on Him* which no one knows except Himself.

13 *He is* clothed with a robe dipped in blood, and His name is called The Word of God.

14 And the armies which are in heaven, clothed in fine linen, white *and* clean, were following Him on white horses.

15 From His mouth comes a sharp sword, so that with it He may strike down the nations, and He will rule them with a rod of iron; and He treads the wine press of the fierce wrath of God, the Almighty.

16 And on His robe and on His thigh He has a name written, "KING OF KINGS, AND LORD OF LORDS."

17 Then I saw an angel standing in the sun, and he cried out with a loud voice, saying to all the birds which fly in midheaven, "Come, assemble for the great supper of God,

18 so that you may eat the flesh of kings and the flesh of commanders and the flesh of mighty men and the flesh of

horses and of those who sit on them and the flesh of all men,

both free men and slaves, and small and great."

19 And I saw the beast and the kings of the earth and their

armies assembled to make war against Him who sat on the

horse and against His army.

20 And the beast was seized, and with him the false prophet

who performed the signs in his presence, by which he

deceived those who had received the mark of the beast and

those who worshiped his image; these two were thrown alive

into the lake of fire which burns with brimstone.

21 And the rest were killed with the sword which came from

the mouth of Him who sat on the horse, and all the birds were

filled with their flesh.

Chapter 20

1 Then I saw an angel coming down from heaven, holding

the key of the abyss and a great chain in his hand.

2 And he laid hold of the dragon, the serpent of old, who is

the devil and Satan, and bound him for a thousand years;

3 and he threw him into the abyss, and shut *it* and sealed *it*

over him, so that he would not deceive the nations any longer, until the thousand years were completed; after these things he must be released for a short time.

4 Then I saw thrones, and they sat on them, and judgment was given to them. And I *saw* the souls of those who had been beheaded because of their testimony of Jesus and because of the word of God, and those who had not worshiped the beast or his image, and had not received the mark on their forehead and on their hand; and they came to life and reigned with Christ for a thousand years.

5 The rest of the dead did not come to life until the thousand years were completed. This is the first resurrection.

6 Blessed and holy is the one who has a part in the first resurrection; over these the second death has no power, but they will be priests of God and of Christ and will reign with Him for a thousand years.

7 When the thousand years are completed, Satan will be released from his prison,

8 and will come out to deceive the nations which are in the four corners of the earth, Gog and Magog, to gather them together for the war; the number of them is like the sand of the seashore.

9 And they came up on the broad plain of the earth and surrounded the camp of the saints and the beloved city, and fire came down from heaven and devoured them.

10 And the devil who deceived them was thrown into the lake of fire and brimstone, where the beast and the false prophet are also; and they will be tormented day and night forever and ever.

11 Then I saw a great white throne and Him who sat upon it, from whose presence earth and heaven fled away, and no place was found for them.

12 And I saw the dead, the great and the small, standing before the throne, and books were opened; and another book was opened, which is *the book* of life; and the dead were judged from the things which were written in the books, according to their deeds.

13 And the sea gave up the dead which were in it, and death and Hades gave up the dead which were in them; and they were judged, every one *of them* according to their deeds.

14 Then death and Hades were thrown into the lake of fire. This is the second death, the lake of fire.

15 And if anyone's name was not found written in the book of life, he was thrown into the lake of fire.

Chapter 21

1 Then I saw a new heaven and a new earth; for the first heaven and the first earth passed away, and there is no longer *any* sea.

2 And I saw the holy city, new Jerusalem, coming down out of heaven from God, made ready as a bride adorned for her husband.

3 And I heard a loud voice from the throne, saying, "Behold, the tabernacle of God is among men, and He will dwell among them, and they shall be His people, and God Himself will be among them,

4 and He will wipe away every tear from their eyes; and there will no longer be *any* death; there will no longer be *any* mourning, or crying, or pain; the first things have passed away."

5 And He who sits on the throne said, "Behold, I am making all things new." And He said, "Write, for these words are faithful and true."

6 Then He said to me, "It is done. I am the Alpha and the

Omega, the beginning and the end. I will give to the one who thirsts from the spring of the water of life without cost.

7 "He who overcomes will inherit these things, and I will be his God and he will be My son.

8 "But for the cowardly and unbelieving and abominable and murderers and immoral persons and sorcerers and idolaters and all liars, their part *will be* in the lake that burns with fire and brimstone, which is the second death."

9 Then one of the seven angels who had the seven bowls full of the seven last plagues came and spoke with me, saying, "Come here, I will show you the bride, the wife of the Lamb."

10 And he carried me away in the Spirit to a great and high mountain, and showed me the holy city, Jerusalem, coming down out of heaven from God,

11having the glory of God. Her brilliance was like a very costly stone, as a stone of crystal-clear jasper.

12 It had a great and high wall, with twelve gates, and at the gates twelve angels; and names *were* written on them, which are *the names* of the twelve tribes of the sons of Israel.

13 *There were* three gates on the east and three gates on the north and three gates on the south and three gates on the west.

14And the wall of the city had twelve foundation stones, and on them *were* the twelve names of the twelve apostles of the Lamb.

15 The one who spoke with me had a gold measuring rod to measure the city, and its gates and its wall.

16 The city is laid out as a square, and its length is as great as the width; and he measured the city with the rod, fifteen hundred miles; its length and width and height are equal.

17 And he measured its wall, seventy-two yards, *according to* human measurements, which are *also* angelic *measurements.*

18 The material of the wall was jasper; and the city was pure gold, like clear glass.

19 The foundation stones of the city wall were adorned with every kind of precious stone. The first foundation stone was jasper; the second, sapphire; the third, chalcedony; the fourth, emerald;

20 the fifth, sardonyx; the sixth, sardius; the seventh, chryso-lite; the eighth, beryl; the ninth, topaz; the tenth, chrysoprase; the eleventh, jacinth; the twelfth, amethyst.

21 And the twelve gates were twelve pearls; each one of the gates was a single pearl. And the street of the city was pure gold, like transparent glass.

22 I saw no temple in it, for the Lord God the Almighty and the Lamb are its temple.

23 And the city has no need of the sun or of the moon to shine on it, for the glory of God has illumined it, and its lamp *is* the Lamb.

24 The nations will walk by its light, and the kings of the earth will bring their glory into it.

25 In the daytime (for there will be no night there) its gates will never be closed;

26 and they will bring the glory and the honor of the nations into it;

27 and nothing unclean, and no one who practices abomination and lying, shall ever come into it, but only those whose names are written in the Lamb's book of life.

Chapter 22

1 Then he showed me a river of the water of life, clear as crystal, coming from the throne of God and of the Lamb,

2 in the middle of its street. On either side of the river was the tree of life, bearing twelve *kinds of* fruit, yielding its fruit every month; and the leaves of the tree were for the healing of the nations.

3 There will no longer be any curse; and the throne of God and of the Lamb will be in it, and His bond-servants will serve Him;

4 they will see His face, and His name *will be* on their foreheads.

5 And there will no longer be *any* night; and they will not have need of the light of a lamp nor the light of the sun, because the Lord God will illumine them; and they will reign forever and ever.

6 And he said to me, "These words are faithful and true"; and the Lord, the God of the spirits of the prophets, sent His angel to show to His bond-servants the things which must soon take place.

7 "And behold, I am coming quickly. Blessed is he who heeds the words of the prophecy of this book."

8 I, John, am the one who heard and saw these things. And when I heard and saw, I fell down to worship at the feet of the angel who showed me these things.

9 But he said to me, "Do not do that. I am a fellow servant of yours and of your brethren the prophets and of those who heed the words of this book. Worship God."

10 And he said to me, "Do not seal up the words of the prophecy of this book, for the time is near.

11 "Let the one who does wrong, still do wrong; and the one who is filthy, still be filthy; and let the one who is righteous, still practice righteousness; and the one who is holy, still keep himself holy."

12 "Behold, I am coming quickly, and My reward *is* with Me, to render to every man according to what he has done.

13 "I am the Alpha and the Omega, the first and the last, the beginning and the end."

14 Blessed are those who wash their robes, so that they may have the right to the tree of life, and may enter by the gates into the city.

15 Outside are the dogs and the sorcerers and the immoral persons and the murderers and the idolaters, and everyone who loves and practices lying.

16 "I, Jesus, have sent My angel to testify to you these things for the churches. I am the root and the descendant of David, the bright morning star."

17 The Spirit and the bride say, "Come." And let the one who hears say, "Come." And let the one who is thirsty come; let the one who wishes take the water of life without cost.

18 I testify to everyone who hears the words of the prophecy of this book: if anyone adds to them, God will add to him the plagues which are written in this book;

19 and if anyone takes away from the words of the book of this prophecy, God will take away his part from the tree of life and from the holy city, which are written in this book.

20 He who testifies to these things says, "Yes, I am coming quickly." Amen. Come, Lord Jesus.

21 The grace of the Lord Jesus be with all. Amen.

*D*o you want a life that thrives?

Wherever you are on your spiritual journey, there is a way to discover Truth for yourself so you can find the abundant life in Christ.

Kay Arthur and Janna Arndt invite you to join them on the ultimate journey. Learn to live life God's way by knowing Him through His Word.

Visit www.precept.org/thrives to take the next step by downloading a free study tool.

PRECEPT MINISTRIES INTERNATIONAL
THE ▼ INDUCTIVE BIBLE STUDY PEOPLE

BRING THE WHOLE COUNSEL OF GOD'S WORD TO KIDS!

▼ GENESIS
God's Amazing Creation (Genesis 1–2)
Digging Up the Past (Genesis 3–11)
Abraham, God's Brave Explorer (Genesis 11–25)
Extreme Adventures with God (Genesis 24–36)
Joseph, God's Superhero (Genesis 37–50)

◄ 2 TIMOTHY
Becoming God's Champion

◄ JAMES
Boy, Have I Got Problems!

ESTHER ▶
God Has Big Plans for You, Esther

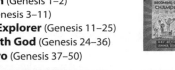

  ◄ REVELATION
Bible Prophecy for Kids
(Revelation 1–7)
A Sneak Peek into the Future
(Revelation 8–22)

DANIEL ▶
You're a Brave Man, Daniel!
(Daniel 1–6)
Fast-Forward to the Future
(Daniel 7–12)

▲ TOPICAL & SKILLS
God, What's Your Name? (Names of God)
Lord, Teach Me to Pray (for Kids)
How to Study Your Bible (for Kids)
 also available in DVD
Cracking the Covenant Code (for Kids)

JONAH ▶
Wrong Way, Jonah!

◄ GOSPEL OF JOHN
Jesus in the Spotlight (John 1–10)
Jesus—Awesome Power, Awesome Love (John 11–16)
Jesus—To Eternity and Beyond (John 17–21)

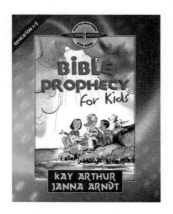

BiBLE PROPHECY FoR KiDS

Are you ready for adventure? Join Max, Molly, and Sam—the amazing beagle—and become an awesome Bible detective! In this intriguing mystery, you'll explore the clues and uncover secrets from the very last book in the Bible. As you look at Revelation 1–7, you'll discover action-packed events, unusual creatures and mind-boggling sights. You'll also find out…

» what heaven is like

» what God says to some special churches—and to you

» what exciting things are going to happen in the future

» what the fantastic rewards of knowing Jesus are

Wow! Enjoy the dynamite discoveries, challenging puzzles, and great hands-on activities in this book. Get ready to have fun and learn how you can live for Jesus today and be prepared for what's to come.